英文

日本 絵 とき事典1

ILLUSTRATED

A LOOK INTO JAPAN

[文化・風俗編]

How to use this book

1) Composition
   The main text is divided into four parts, that is,
   "Traditional Culture", "Life and Customs",
   "Food" and "Travel". You can read this book
   in any order you like. A chronological table and
   additional information are attached at the end
   of this book for your convenience.

2) Lettering
   All Japanese words that appear in this book are
   in the Hepburn System of Romanization and as
   a general rule, when they appear in the text
   they are in italics. (However, this does not apply
   to headings and bold type.)
   In addition, long vowels have a solid line above
   (Ex. Shintō) and e's at the end of words which
   are pronounced have accents above (Ex. Saké).

Dear Readers:

Visitors often express disappointment at finding Japan so "Westernized." Many are convinced that the country's remarkable economic success has come only at the expense of its culture.

There is no question that modernity has effected a number of far reaching and profound changes upon Japan and its people. But a closer look reveals that, beneath the industrialized, Westernized surface, virtually every aspect of Japanese life remains firmly rooted in tradition. Most traditional arts are still very much alive, centuries-old customs still play an important role in society and business, and "things Japanese," from the mundane to the sublime, still abound in everyday life.

This book has been designed to familiarize readers with a basic concept related to a wide variety of Japanese arts, customs, and lifestyles. The generous use of illustrations has eliminated the need for wordy explanations and will, it is hoped, aid the reader in retaining and recalling the vocabulary for any given section. Additional information on certain items is also provided in the supplementary pages.

We believe that "A LOOK INTO JAPAN" will help you to better appreciate and understand the real Japan, and to communicate more effectively during your stay.

CONTENTS

Traditional Culture ——————— 伝統・文化

伝統・文化

Architecture

The distinctive feature of traditional Japanese building is the way in which the house is open to nature. The main materials used are wood, earth, and paper, and the construction spreads out sideways rather than upwards.

■ Traditional houses

Tateana-shiki, or pit-style, dwelling *(Yayoi* era)

Takayuka-shiki dwelling, used mainly for warehouses

Thatched roof

Tiled roof

Plaster wall

Doma, or dirt-floored room

Farm house

Merchant's house

This style of farmhouse remains unchanged to the present day

The steep pitch of the roof is to prevent snow from accumulating

This style can be seen in Takayama (Gifu prefecture)

Gasshō-zukuri style

Corridor enclosing the central garden

Shinden-zukuri

Nobleman's house in the *Heian* era.

* Shoin zukuri

Official's (nobleman or *samurai*) house after the *Shinden-zukuri* period.

■ Modern housing

With the steady flow of population into the cities, the price of land went up rapidly, and Japanese-style houses with gardens became prohibitively expensive for most people. This led to a great increase in the number of apartment houses and duplexes.

Only narrow spaces between houses.

Ready-built houses. Standardized housing has become a common sight.

A *Danchi*, or housing complex

---

* For interior of *shoin-zukuri* bldg. see page 160 et seq.

One of the features of Japanese houses is the tremendous variety of roof styles, depending on the locality and the occupation of the owner. These styles can, however, be classified roughly into three styles called *Yosemunē*, *Kirizuma* and *Irimoya*.

Names of roof components

Various materials are used in the construction of roofs, including *Kaya* (a kind of reed), wheat straw, bamboo, tiles, stone, galvanized iron, and aluminium.

Types of roof

Roof styles

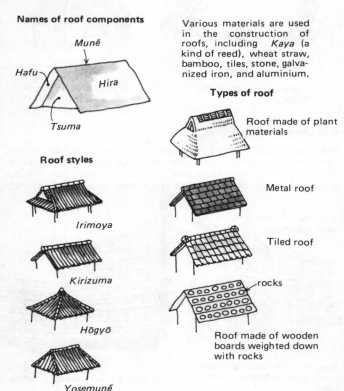

Munē

Hafu

Hira

Tsuma

Roof made of plant materials

Metal roof

Irimoya

Kirizuma

Tiled roof

Hōgyō

rocks

Yosemunē

Roof made of wooden boards weighted down with rocks

Types of roof tiles

Karakusa -gawara *Ichimonji -karakusa -gawara* *Sodé-gawara* *Maru -gawara* *Oni-gawara* *Tomoé- gawara*

Recently, Japanese cities have come to look like those of Europe because of the increase in the number of prefabricated and ferroconcrete buildings. However, the style of building that is best suited to the Japanese climate and natural conditions is probably still the traditional wooden house, and it is certainly nicer to look at.

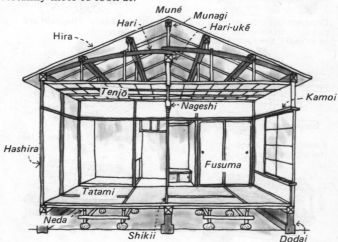

Construction of a small wooden house in the traditional style.

11

How to build a wooden house

Jinawabari: Ropes are stretched out on the site to mark the position of the house.

Concrete-uchi: Shuttering is put up, and concrete is poured in to make the foundations.

Kizami: The wood for the frame is cut to size.

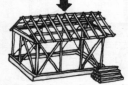

Jōtō: The frame is erected on the foundations.

Yanefuki: The roof is tiled.

Kabenuri: The walls are plastered.

Yukabari: The floor is laid.

Shiagé: The house is completed.

This is the layout of a so-called 2LDK apartment (this means an apartment with two living rooms also used as bedrooms, a dining-room and a kitchen, the last two usually being combined into one). This would be for a family of three; mother, father and one child.

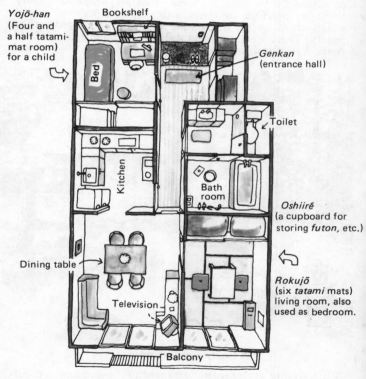

Yojō-han
(Four and a half tatami-mat room) for a child

Bookshelf

Bed

Genkan
(entrance hall)

Toilet

Kitchen

Bath room

Oshiiré
(a cupboard for storing *futon,* etc.)

Dining table

Television

Rokujō
(six *tatami* mats) living room, also used as bedroom.

Balcony

Layout of an average apartment in the city.

庭園　Garden

The Japanese garden is designed to be a faithful representation of nature and to impart a sense of simple, unspoiled beauty. Its style therefore contrasts with that of a Western garden, which relies on shaping nature into a kind of geometrical beauty. There are three main styles of Japanese garden; *Tsukiyama, Karesansui,* and *Chaniwa.*

Tea-house
(See page 32.)

This area represents the sea.

A Tsukiyama-style garden

A *'Tsukiyama'*-style garden is arranged to show nature in miniature, with hills, ponds and streams.

The *Karesansui* style of garden developed in the *Muromachi* Era as a representation of *Zen* spiritualism (See P.66).
In this style, sand or gravel is used to represent rivers or the sea. It is characterized by its force and simplicity.

The flow of water is represented by white sand.

Karesansui-style garden (The Ryōanji rock garden at Kyōto)

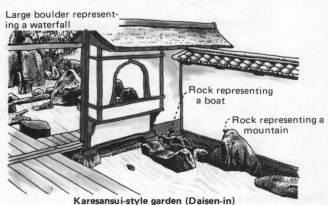

Large boulder representing a waterfall

Rock representing a boat

Rock representing a mountain

Karesansui-style garden (Daisen-in)

The *Chaniwa* is the garden adjacent to a ceremonial teahouse. This style of garden avoids any suggestion of showiness and strives for the utmost simplicity and naturalness. The main features of such a garden are shown here:

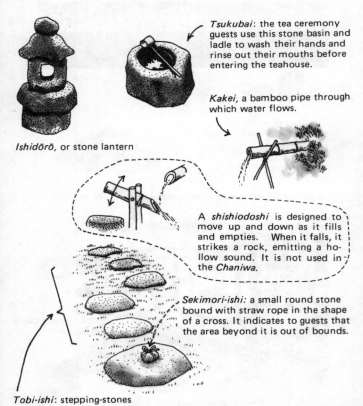

Tsukubai: the tea ceremony guests use this stone basin and ladle to wash their hands and rinse out their mouths before entering the teahouse.

Kakei, a bamboo pipe through which water flows.

Ishidōrō, or stone lantern

A *shishiodoshi* is designed to move up and down as it fills and empties. When it falls, it strikes a rock, emitting a hollow sound. It is not used in the *Chaniwa*.

Sekimori-ishi: a small round stone bound with straw rope in the shape of a cross. It indicates to guests that the area beyond it is out of bounds.

Tobi-ishi: stepping-stones

城　Castle

Castles in Japan underwent their most intensive phase of development in the *Sengoku* (Warring States) era from the 15th to the 16th century. Built with the object of keeping the enemy out, they are elaborate in design and strongly fortified. Their magnificent architecture also served to demonstrate the power of the *jōshu*, or lord of the castle.

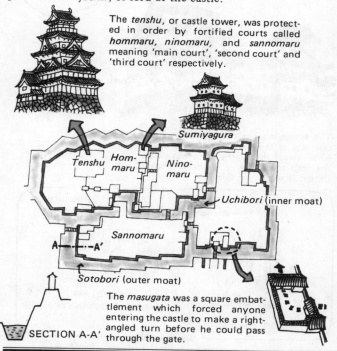

The *tenshu*, or castle tower, was protected in order by fortified courts called *hommaru*, *ninomaru*, and *sannomaru* meaning 'main court', 'second court' and 'third court' respectively.

Sumiyagura

Tenshu　Hom-maru　Nino-maru

Uchibori (inner moat)

Sannomaru

A' - - - A'

Sotobori (outer moat)

SECTION A-A'

The *masugata* was a square embattlement which forced anyone entering the castle to make a right-angled turn before he could pass through the gate.

17

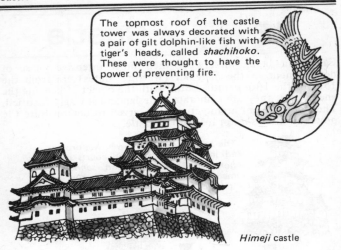

The topmost roof of the castle tower was always decorated with a pair of gilt dolphin-like fish with tiger's heads, called *shachihoko*. These were thought to have the power of preventing fire.

Himeji castle

The *tenshu* was the stronghold and headquarters of the castle, and the place of final retreat in a battle. This was where the lord of the castle would live when the castle was under siege.

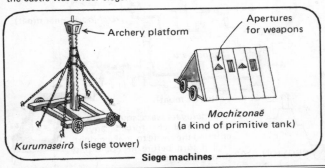

Archery platform

Apertures for weapons

Kurumaseirō (siege tower)

Mochizonaē (a kind of primitive tank)

Siege machines

Details of castle construction

Jūgan, or loophole. Various devices were used to make the castle more secure against an attacker. The castle tower and watchtowers were provided with loopholes through which guns could be fired *(jūgan)* or arrows shot *(yumihazama)*.

Loophole in a wall. The inner opening is enlarged so as to facilitate observation of the outside.

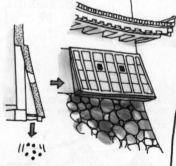

Ishiotoshi. This was a special chamber built out over the wall of the castle. Its floor could be opened downwards to drop rocks onto the heads of attackers trying to scale the walls.

As explained above, it was very difficult to capture a castle. So there were men called *ninja*, specially trained in the art of being unseen. In the picture, one is trying to sneak into the castle.

神社 Shintō Shrine

The *Jinja*, or shrine, is where believers in Japan's indigenous religion, *Shintō*, go to worship. *Shintō* originated in ancient peoples' fears of demons and supernatural powers, and their worship of these. It has no written body of doctrine, but it is Japan's main religion and is practised widely through ceremonies and festivals.

阿
A

Komainu: These are the stone dogs which face each other at the entrance to shrines, guarding the precincts. One dog always has its mouth open and is called *A*, while the other has its mouth closed and is called *Un*.

吽
Un

Inari style - *torii*

The symbol of a shrine is its gate, or *Torii*. It represents the division between the everyday world and the divine world.

--- *Hishaku*
(ladle)

-- Water

Chōzuya. The small pavilion near the main hall with water and ladles is called the *Chōzuya*. People come here to wash their hands and rinse out their mouths before going to the main hall to pray.

The main sanctuary of a shrine (*Tōshōgū*)

■Shrine architecture

The main sanctuary of a shrine is called the *Shinden* or *Honden*. There are also ancillary buildings such as the *Haiden*, or outer hall, and the *Hōmotsuden*, or treasury, but these are not arranged according to any particular specified layout.

Main honden styles

Katsuogi
Chigi
Iraka-ōi
Munamochi-bashira
Kiza-hashi

Shinmei-zukuri:
Isé Jingū (Mié Prefecture)

Sumiyoshi-zukuri:
Sumiyoshi Taisha (Ōsaka)

Kasuga-zukuri:
Kasuga Taisha (Nara)

Taisha-zukuri:
Izumo Taisha (Shimané Prefecture)

Hachiman-zukuri:
Usa Jingū (Ōita Prefecture)

Nagaré-zukuri:
Kamo Jinja (Kyōto)

There are many lucky charms and other such objects to be seen at a shrine. Some are used to determine the will of the gods, and some as a way of communicating with the gods and asking for their protection.

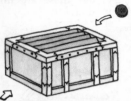

Ema: a wooden votive tablet with a picture of a horse, the divine steed, on it.

Saisen-bako: the *Saisen-bako* is a collection box into which people throw money as a way of expressing their gratitude for divine favours received or of showing their sincerity when asking for such favours.

Omikuji: a fortune written on a piece of paper and selected by shaking a bamboo stick from a box. The slip of paper is then tied to the branch of a tree in the shrine grounds. Fortunes are classified into *Daikichi* (great good fortune), *Kichi* (good fortune), *Shōkichi* (moderate good fortune) and *Kyō* (bad luck).

* *Suzu:* a bell rung by worshippers to announce to the god of the shrine that they have come to pray.

Omamori: a special talisman thought to be imbued with the power to bring good luck and ward off evil.

22

* *Suzu*: See page 83.

The chief priest of a shrine is called the *Kannushi*. He is responsible for all the religious observances and the running of the shrine. The young girl assistants in a shrine are called *Miko*.

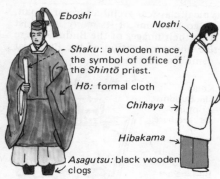

Eboshi

Shaku: a wooden mace, the symbol of office of the *Shintō* priest.

Hō: formal cloth

Noshi

Chihaya

Hibakama

Asagutsu: black wooden clogs

Kan-nushi

The chief priest's vestments are called *Ikan* (see picture), and as well as this he has a *Kariginu* (white robes with a coloured *hakama*) for everyday wear, and a *Jōi*, which is all white.

Miko

In ancient times, it was believed that people died when the soul left the body. To try and call it back, they used a form of magic called *Kagura*, which involved dancing and playing flutes and drums. This became formalized and developed into *Noh* and *Kyōgen*.

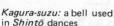

Kagura-suzu: a bell used in *Shintō* dances

Kagura masks

Okamé: the mask of a young, jolly-faced, attractive woman

Hyottoko: a droll-faced man's mask. His lips are pursed because he often breathes fire and tells lies.

23

寺院 Buddhist Temple

If you want to see the typical classical architecture of Japan, there is no better place to go than one of its many Buddhist temples. These temples, with their images of the Buddha, were established for the practice and propagation of the Buddhist religion, which originally came from India.

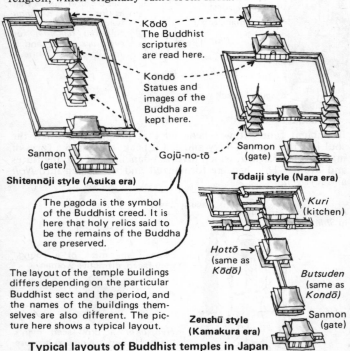

Kōdō
The Buddhist scriptures are read here.

Kondō
Statues and images of the Buddha are kept here.

Sanmon (gate)

Gojū-no-tō

Shitennōji style (Asuka era)

Sanmon (gate)

Tōdaiji style (Nara era)

The pagoda is the symbol of the Buddhist creed. It is here that holy relics said to be the remains of the Buddha are preserved.

Kuri (kitchen)

Hottō → (same as *Kōdō*)

Butsuden (same as *Kondō*)

Sanmon (gate)

The layout of the temple buildings differs depending on the particular Buddhist sect and the period, and the names of the buildings themselves are also different. The picture here shows a typical layout.

Zenshū style (Kamakura era)

Typical layouts of Buddhist temples in Japan

Various features of temple architecture

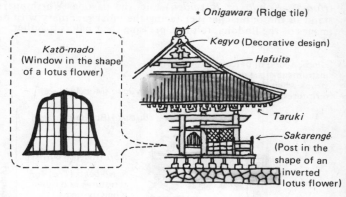

Katō-mado
(Window in the shape of a lotus flower)

* *Onigawara* (Ridge tile)

Kegyo (Decorative design)

Hafuita

Taruki

Sakarengé
(Post in the shape of an inverted lotus flower)

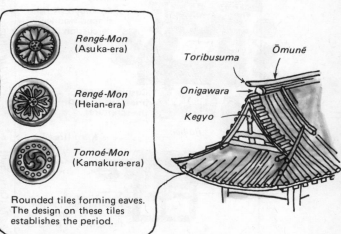

Rengé-Mon
(Asuka-era)

Rengé-Mon
(Heian-era)

Tomoé-Mon
(Kamakura-era)

Rounded tiles forming eaves. The design on these tiles establishes the period.

Toribusuma

Ōmuné

Onigawara

Kegyo

---

* *Onigawara:* See page 11.

Buddhist temple

The most important buildings in the temple are the main hall (*Hondō*, *Kondō* or *Butsuden*) and the pagoda. Worshippers stand in the outer chamber facing the inner sanctuary, with its images of the Buddha, to pray, pressing their palms together.

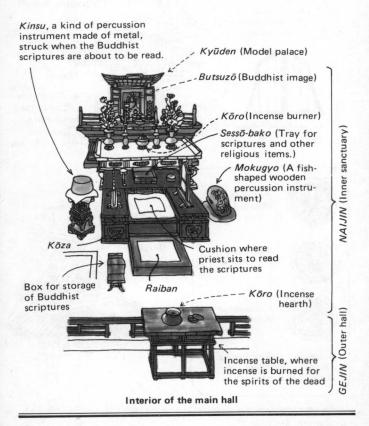

Kinsu, a kind of percussion instrument made of metal, struck when the Buddhist scriptures are about to be read.

Kyūden (Model palace)

Butsuzō (Buddhist image)

Kōro (Incense burner)

Sessō-bako (Tray for scriptures and other religious items.)

Mokugyo (A fish-shaped wooden percussion instrument)

NAIJIN (Inner sanctuary)

Kōza

Cushion where priest sits to read the scriptures

Box for storage of Buddhist scriptures

Raiban

Kōro (Incense hearth)

GEJIN (Outer hall)

Incense table, where incense is burned for the spirits of the dead

Interior of the main hall

In India, the temple building which houses what are said to be the remains of the Buddha is called a stupa. In its passage to Japan via China and Korea, this type of building changed its shape and became the five-storied pagoda of the typical Japanese temple.

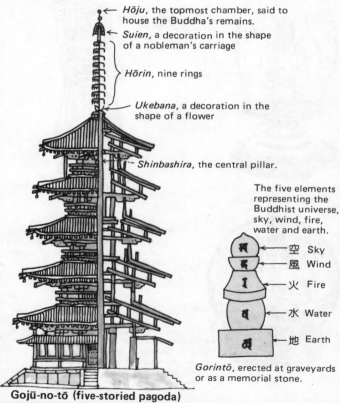

← *Hōju*, the topmost chamber, said to house the Buddha's remains.

← *Suien*, a decoration in the shape of a nobleman's carriage

Hōrin, nine rings

← *Ukebana*, a decoration in the shape of a flower

Shinbashira, the central pillar.

The five elements representing the Buddhist universe, sky, wind, fire, water and earth.

空 Sky
風 Wind
火 Fire
水 Water
地 Earth

Gorintō, erected at graveyards or as a memorial stone.

Gojū-no-tō (five-storied pagoda)

27

A statue representing the Buddha

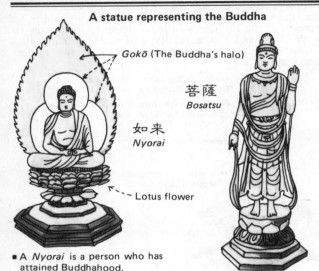

Gokō (The Buddha's halo)

菩薩
Bosatsu

如来
Nyorai

Lotus flower

- A *Nyorai* is a person who has attained Buddhahood.

- A *Bosatsu*, or bodhisattva, is a lay person who is undergoing religious training with the object of attaining Buddhahood.

明王 *Myō-ō*

- *Myō-ō* is an envoy of the Buddha sent to fight evil. He usually has a large number of arms, eyes or heads and looks weird and frightening.

The position of the Buddha's hands and legs

Insō, or hand positions

Gōmaza   *Kissōza*   *Hankafuza*

The position of the Buddha's legs
shows his stage of attainment.

Bonshō

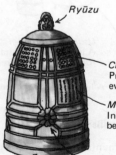

Ryūzu

The *Bonshō* is the Buddhist temple
bell. It is struck 108 times on New
Year's Eve to ring in the New Year
and drive out the 108 evil desires
that man is heir to. *(Joya-no-kané)*

Chichi:
Projections representing the 108
evil desires

Mei-bun:
Inscription giving the history of the
bell or listing supplications.

Tsukiza: The point which the clap-
per strikes, with a lotus-petal design

Komanotsumé

茶の湯　Tea Ceremony

Cha-no-yu (the tea ceremony) or *Sadō* (lit. the way of tea) was introduced to Japan from China and perfected by Master *Sen-no-Rikyū* based on the spirit of *Zen* in the 16th century.

Kama & Furo (Kettle & Brazier):
The *kama,* which contains the water, is placed on the *furo* to boil. (In the winter, a *ro,* or inset hearth, is exposed by removing part of the floor-boards)

Mizusashi: A jug. The water in the *mizusashi* is used to wash the *chawan* (teacup) or poured into the *kama.*

Kama

Furo

Kensui

Chawan: A tea cup or tea bowl.

Usuki or *Natsumé:* A lacquerware container for *usucha* (powdered tea).

Kensui: A pot in which the water used to wash the *chawan* is poured.

Hishaku: A ladle to pour the water.

▲ Cha-no-yu Utensils

For Japanese people, *cha-no-yu* is a mental discipline for pursuing *"*wabi*"(a state of mind in which a person is calm and content, with a profound simplicity), and is at the same time a performance in which form and grace are paramount.

* *Wabi:* See page 182.

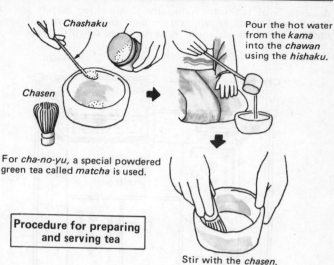

Chashaku

Chasen

Pour the hot water from the *kama* into the *chawan* using the *hishaku*.

For *cha-no-yu*, a special powdered green tea called *matcha* is used.

Stir with the *chasen*.

Procedure for preparing and serving tea

Bow and receive the *chawan* with the right hand, and place it on the palm of the left hand.

Rotate the *chawan* clockwise three times with the right hand.

After drinking the tea, wipe the part of the *chawan* which the lips touched with the right hand, and rotate the *chawan* counterclockwise, then return it to the host.

How to drink the tea and return it to the host.

A ceremonial tea-room is usually about three meters square (a four-and-a-half *tatami*-mat room), and is decorated very simply. The spirit of *"wabi"* is exemplified by this tea-room.

■ **Ceremonial tea-room**

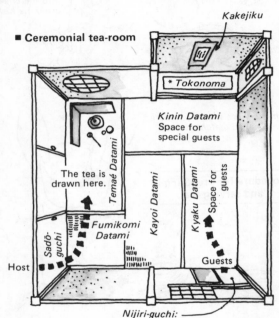

Kakejiku

* *Tokonoma*

Kinin Datami
Space for special guests

The tea is drawn here.

Temaé Datami

Kayoi Datami

Kyaku Datami
Space for guests

Fumikomi Datami

Sadō-guchi

Host

Guests

Nijiri-guchi:
A side door about 60 cm square through which guests enter the tea-room. Since they are forced to bow when passing through this door, they naturally lose their sense of self-importance and become humble.

The style of *cha-no-yu* depends on the school, such as *Ura-Senké, Omoté-Senké,* etc. The style described above is primarily that of *Ura-Senké.*

* *Tokonoma:* See page 160.

地蔵・道祖神　Jizō, Dōsojin

Jizō are very familiar objects of folk belief in Japan, and are made from sculpted stone. There are various types of *jizō*, but most of them are icons dedicated to the divine protection of children.

Shakujō

Hōju

Kesa

Jizō-bosatsu, who relieves people from suffering and distress.

Dōsojin is a roadside icon usually placed at a street corner or at the foot of a bridge to protect pedestrians.

Koyasu-jizō, who is holding a baby.

A *dōsojin* of marriage

生け花 | Floral Art

Japanese floral art *(ikebana)* was brought to its peak of refinement in the latter half of the sixteenth century by its founder, *Sen-no-Rikyū*. At present, there are about three thousand schools of *ikebana*, two of the better-known ones being the *Ikenobō* school and the *Ohara* school.

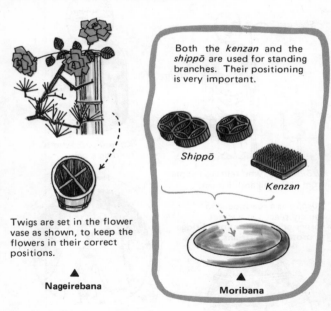

Both the *kenzan* and the *shippō* are used for standing branches. Their positioning is very important.

Shippō

Kenzan

Twigs are set in the flower vase as shown, to keep the flowers in their correct positions.

▲
Nageirebana

▲
Moribana

Ikebana can be divided into two main styles, *nageirebana* and *moribana*, depending on the type of vase used.

The flowers can be arranged in the various styles shown below. Particular styles are best suited to particular flowers.

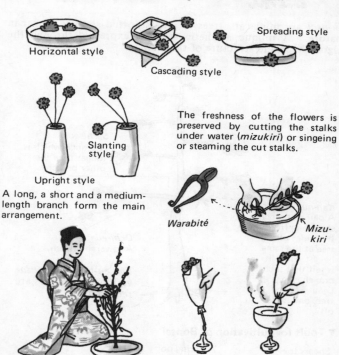

Horizontal style

Cascading style

Spreading style

Slanting style

Upright style

A long, a short and a medium-length branch form the main arrangement.

The freshness of the flowers is preserved by cutting the stalks under water (*mizukiri*) or singeing or steaming the cut stalks.

Warabité

Mizu-kiri

Along with the tea ceremony, *ikebana* is very popular among young Japanese women, and there are many schools where they can go to learn it. In modern schools, teaching styles are sometimes very different from the traditional ones shown here. The *Sōgetsu* school is one of the popular modern schools.

盆栽　Bonsai

Bonsai are miniature trees or plants potted as they appear in nature. A unique aesthetic sense is expressed through the vigor, shape and structure of the plant.

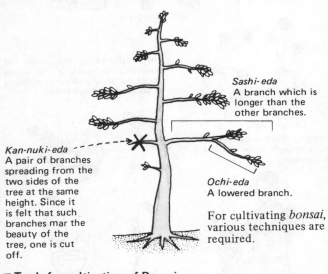

Sashi-eda
A branch which is longer than the other branches.

Kan-nuki-eda
A pair of branches spreading from the two sides of the tree at the same height. Since it is felt that such branches mar the beauty of the tree, one is cut off.

Ochi-eda
A lowered branch.

For cultivating *bonsai*, various techniques are required.

▼ Tools for cultivation of Bonsai

Shears for root cutting

Watering pot

Saw

Wire

Pruning shears　Hemp-palm broom

■ Typical tree shapes

Chokkan: An upright tree.

Kengai: A tree which appears to be hanging from a cliff toward a gorge.

Ishizuki: A *bonsai* whose root clings to rocks. Certain *bonsai* are rooted on rocks in this way.

Bunjingi: a graceful curved shape

焼きもの　Pottery

Pottery *(Yakimono)* provides useful articles and objects of art at the same time. The pottery made in various periods and districts in Japan has distinctive features.

The aesthetic sense and life of the period and district where it was made can be seen in the pottery itself.

Rokuro:
Pots are usually shaped on a potter's wheel. This wheel is turned with the feet or hands, or by an electric motor.

Suyaki:
After being shaped on the wheel, the pot is dried naturally and fired without glazing.

The pot is finally fired at a temperature suitable for its glaze.

Etsuké:
Pictures are drawn directly on the pot, which is then glazed.

▲ **Pottery-making**

■ Pottery Map

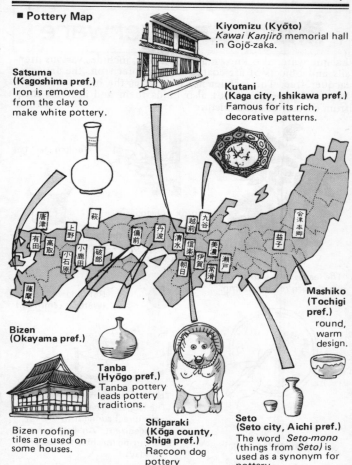

Kiyomizu (Kyōto)
Kawai Kanjirō memorial hall in Gojō-zaka.

Satsuma (Kagoshima pref.)
Iron is removed from the clay to make white pottery.

Kutani (Kaga city, Ishikawa pref.)
Famous for its rich, decorative patterns.

Mashiko (Tochigi pref.)
round, warm design.

Bizen (Okayama pref.)

Bizen roofing tiles are used on some houses.

Tanba (Hyōgo pref.)
Tanba pottery leads pottery traditions.

Shigaraki (Kōga county, Shiga pref.)
Raccoon dog pottery

Seto (Seto city, Aichi pref.)
The word *Seto-mono* (things from *Seto*) is used as a synonym for pottery.

漆器 Lacquerware

Lacquerware, also known as Japanware, includes various utensils and objects of art coated with lacquer from the Japanese lacquer tree. The lacquer not only gives the basic materials a beautiful appearance but also binds them and protects them from corrosives and moisture.

Hooked steel bar

Trunk of lacquer tree.

A cut is made in the bark of the *urushi* tree, and the drops of sap are collected. This is the raw lacquer.

The leaves of the *urushi* tree, which turn red in autumn.

Refining
(Water is removed.)

The process of *nayashi* work
(The lacquer is heated and stirred under direct sunlight to homogenize it. An electric heater and stirring machine are used nowadays.)

Making the design

Wood, leather, paper, porcelain and metal are used as the basic materials.

The lacquer is usually applied in three coats; undercoat, middle coat, and top coat.

Wajima lacquerware from Ishikawa prefecture is one of the most famous types.

Wajima lacquerware

Shunkei lacquerware: wooden ware dyed yellow or red, then coated with lacquer. (Kiso lacquerware from Nagano prefecture is the best-known of this type.)

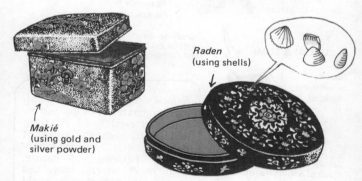

Raden
(using shells)

Makié
(using gold and
silver powder)

To decorate lacquerware, techniques such as using gold and silver powder or inlaying with mother-of-pearl or other shells are used.

書画　Calligraphy & Sumi-é

Sho, or calligraphy, is one of the unique arts of the East. In it, beauty is sought through the shape and position of the characters drawn, the gradation of the ink, and the force of the brush-strokes.

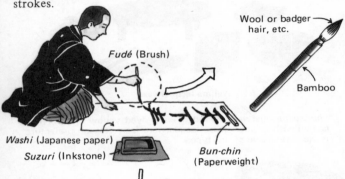

Wool or badger hair, etc.

Fudé (Brush)

Bamboo

Washi (Japanese paper)

Suzuri (Inkstone)

Bun-chin (Paperweight)

Suzuri-no-umi (well of inkstone, hollowed out to hold water)

● SUZURI & SUMI

Suzuri, or inkstone, made of stone.

Sumi (Ink)

Sumi, or India-ink stick, is made of a mixture of lamp-black or plant soot and glue. Ink is produced when this is rubbed with water on the inkstone.

Suiboku-ga, or India-ink paintings, originated in China and became an established art form mainly through the work of painter priests. They are mono-chrome paintings of nature, with rocks, rivers, trees and mountains, depicting a world of contemplation and meditation.

Perspective is shown by the shading of the ink.

The composition has depth but no focal point.

If people are present, they are depicted as part of nature and blend into the scene.

SUIBOKU-GA

43

道具・骨董品 Folk Objects & Curios

The articles shown here are rarely used today. However, they include some fine examples of the craftsman's skill, and many of them are considered objects of art.

- **Travel kit**

Medicines

← *Sando-gasa*, a hat made from sedge.

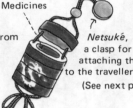

Netsuké, a clasp for attaching things to the traveller's belt (See next page.)

Inrō, a case for holding medicines

↑ *Kappa*, a kind of cape

↑ A gourd used as a water bottle

A bamboo box for food

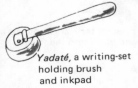

Yadaté, a writing-set holding brush and inkpad

These are some of the things that travellers used to take with them on their journeys in the *Edo* era. As well as being extremely practical, they include some beautiful examples of folk art. They can be seen in historical films of this period.

Netsuké were originally intended to keep tobacco holders or medicine cases on the belt, but they have become prized by collectors abroad because of their unique, detailed designs.

Bizarre design

Netsuké are carved from wood, bamboo, ivory and other materials.

- ## Furniture and household goods.
  (Some of these are still used in country districts today).

Wicker basket, made from bamboo, for clothes

Tansu, or chest

Tsuitaté, or blind

Sentaku-ita, or washing-board, for scrubbing laundry

Seiro, or rice steamer

The lamp is lit inside here.

Japanese paper →

Andon, or lampstand

Karakasa, an oiled paper umbrella with a bamboo framework

Oké, a wooden washtub

■ Craftsmen's tools and equipment

The tools shown here are carpenter's tools, used in the construction of wooden buildings.

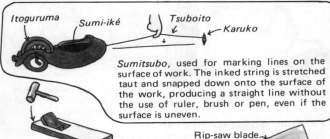

Itoguruma   Sumi-iké   Tsuboito   Karuko

Sumitsubo, used for marking lines on the surface of work. The inked string is stretched taut and snapped down onto the surface of the work, producing a straight line without the use of ruler, brush or pen, even if the surface is uneven.

Kanna, or plane. The length of the exposed blade is adjusted by striking this part with a hammer.

Rip-saw blade

Crosscut blade

Nokogiri, or handsaw.

Japanese planes and saws work in the opposite direction to Western ones, cutting when pulled in towards the body.

Kebiki, or marking gauge. The blade draws a line on the work.

■ For transporting materials

Daihachi-guruma, (handcart)

Shoiko, a frame for carrying things on the back

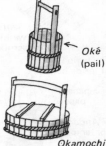

Oké (pail)

Okamochi (for delivering cooked food)

- **Combs and accessories**

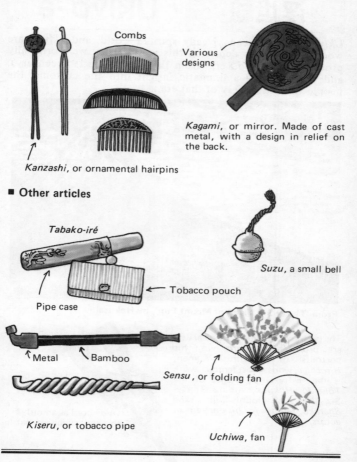

Combs

Various designs

Kagami, or mirror. Made of cast metal, with a design in relief on the back.

Kanzashi, or ornamental hairpins

- **Other articles**

Tabako-iré

Tobacco pouch

Pipe case

Suzu, a small bell

Metal Bamboo

Sensu, or folding fan

Kiseru, or tobacco pipe

Uchiwa, fan

浮世絵　Ukiyo-é

Ukiyo literally means a gaily spirited world, and *ukiyoé* are wood-block prints depicting this world. They were originally produced in the *Edo* era (from the 17th to the 19th century), and they provide a dramatic insight into the customs, the people and the scenery of that era.

From 'Thirty-Six Views of Mount Fuji', by Hokusai.

The best-known of the *ukiyoé* artists are probably *Utamaro*, with his portraits of beautiful women; *Hiroshigé,* whose most famous work is the 'Fifty-Three Stages of the *Tōkaidō';* *Hokusai,* with his 'Thirty-Six Views of Mount Fuji' ; and *Sharaku, famous for his portraits of actors.*

Ukiyoé used as an old-fashioned Japanese battle-dore.

Ukiyoé was a popular art form which appealed to the emotions. People rushed to buy the latest prints of popular actors, beauties and famous courtesans. There were also many erotic prints called *makura-é*.

Producing an Ukiyoé print

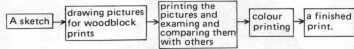

A sketch → drawing pictures for woodblock prints → printing the pictures and examing and comparing them with others → colour printing → a finished print.

絵師

The *eshi,* or painter, sketches the basic design, draws pictures for the woodblock prints and indicates the colors according to the order from the *Ukiyoé* original sellers.

彫師

The *horishi,* or carver, pastes the picture for a print upside-down on a convex carving block, carves the block for a proofsheet in black and white, then carves other blocks for the colors that the painter has designated.

Sharaku, a unique *Ukiyoé* artist, drew characters in his own unique impressionistic style.

■ **Carving tools**

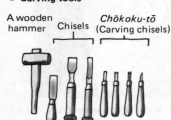

A wooden hammer   Chisels   *Chōkoku-tō* (Carving chisels)

* Cherry wood is used for blocks.

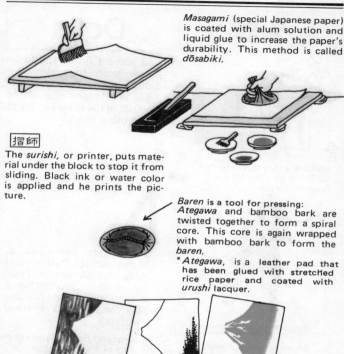

Masagami (special Japanese paper) is coated with alum solution and liquid glue to increase the paper's durability. This method is called *dōsabiki*.

摺師

The *surishi,* or printer, puts material under the block to stop it from sliding. Black ink or water color is applied and he prints the picture.

Baren is a tool for pressing: *Ategawa* and bamboo bark are twisted together to form a spiral core. This core is again wrapped with bamboo bark to form the *baren*.

Ategawa, is a leather pad that has been glued with stretched rice paper and coated with *urushi* lacquer.

Color blocks printed with individual color.

Finish of *Ukiyoé*:
Unique techniques such as blind prints and gradation are extensively used. These techniques cannot be seen in woodblock prints of other countries.

人形	Dolls

In ancient times, the Japanese used to make clay dolls, paper dolls, etc. for use in religious rites or for burial in the tombs of kings and other nobles.

Haniwa, a clay figure found buried in a sixth-century nobleman's tomb.

Straw figure used mainly for religious rites.

Samurai doll displayed on Boys' Festival, May 5th.

Dolls were developed as ornaments for festivals and religious observances. Typical of these are the *hinaningyō* dolls put on display for the Girls' Festival on March 3rd.

Emperor and Empress dolls in the costume of the middle ages. Many of these dolls are clad in gorgeous silk costumes decorated with gold and silver threads.

52

* *Hinaningyō:* See page 84.

Dolls are made locally as objects of art or toys all over Japan. There is a huge variety of styles and materials.

The head rotates.

Beautiful baked finish

Gosho doll (Kyōto)

Hakata doll (Fukuoka)

Saga doll

Gosho dolls were originally made as presents to decorate the Imperial Palace. *Saga* dolls are the richly-coloured dolls first made by the sculptors of Buddhist images. *Kyō* dolls are famous for their gorgeous, specially-woven costumes, and *Hakata* dolls for their beautiful baked finish. The most typical of all the Japanese dolls are the cylindrical wooden *Kokeshi* dolls, found in various districts all over Japan.

Kyō doll (Kyōto)

Kokeshi dolls

楽器　Musical Instruments

Ancient Japanese music has several styles, such as *gagaku* (ancient court music), *nōgaku* (the music played in *Noh* dramas), and *sōkyoku (koto* music). Some of the instruments used in these styles are introduced here.

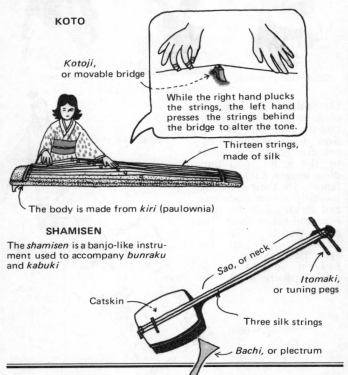

KOTO

Kotoji, or movable bridge

While the right hand plucks the strings, the left hand presses the strings behind the bridge to alter the tone.

Thirteen strings, made of silk

The body is made from *kiri* (paulownia)

SHAMISEN

The *shamisen* is a banjo-like instrument used to accompany *bunraku* and *kabuki*

Sao, or neck

Itomaki, or tuning pegs

Catskin

Three silk strings

Bachi, or plectrum

SHAKUHACHI

The *shakuhachi* and the *yokobué* are types of flute. The *shakuhachi* consists of a bamboo pipe about twenty inches long, and has no reed.

Shakuhachi

Yokobué

A *komusō*, or mendicant *Zen* priest (15th – 16th century), playing a *shakuhachi*.

Instruments used in gagaku.

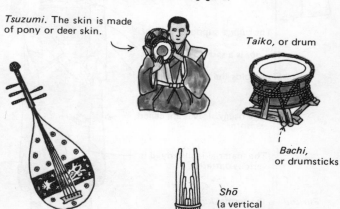

Tsuzumi. The skin is made of pony or deer skin.

Taiko, or drum

Bachi, or drumsticks

Shō (a vertical bamboo flute)

Biwa

着物・帯　Traditional Costume

The *kimono* is the traditional dress of Japan, and it is worn nowadays on formal occasions. It is sometimes accused of being an impractical form of dress, but it has the advantage of giving the wearer a graceful and elegant deportment.

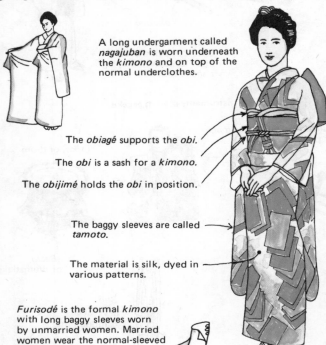

A long undergarment called *nagajuban* is worn underneath the *kimono* and on top of the normal underclothes.

The *obiagé* supports the *obi*.

The *obi* is a sash for a *kimono*.

The *obijimé* holds the *obi* in position.

The baggy sleeves are called *tamoto*.

The material is silk, dyed in various patterns.

Furisodé is the formal *kimono* with long baggy sleeves worn by unmarried women. Married women wear the normal-sleeved *tomesodé*.

Tabi

Men's Kimono are mainly black.

The *montsuki* or *haori*, a half-coat, emblazoned with the wearer's family crest. (See p.60 Family Crests)

Mon (crest)

Sensu, or folding fan

Hakama, a culotte-like garment worn over the *kimono*.

Tabi should be worn with *montsuki*.

Formal wear

The *obi* is made either of stiff material (the *kaku-obi*) or of soft material (the *heko-obi*).

Less formal wear

There are various different types of *kimono* for use at different times and on different occasions. Women's *kimono* include the *furisodé* and *tomesodé* for formal wear, the *hōmongi* for paying calls, the *tsukesagé*, and the *komon*. Men's *kimono* include the *montsuki hakama* for ceremonial occasions, and the *haori* for going out visiting. There is also the *yukata*, worn by both men and women as informal dress at home, in *ryokan* or for attending local festivals.

The shape of the *kimono* is fixed, and individuality is achieved by careful selection of the material, the style of weaving and dyeing, the color, and the pattern, as well as by the choice of *obi*.

Ōshima-tsumugi   Yūzen   Komon

Kimono material, called *tanmono,* is produced in lengths of *ittan* (about 11 m).

- **OBI**

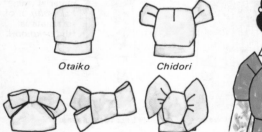

Otaiko   Chidori

Bunko   Kai-no-kuchi   Tateya

Fukurasuzumé

The *obi* is an important part of the overall appearance of the *kimono*, and it can be tied in various ways.

- **OBIJIMÉ**

For happy occasions — congratulations | For ordinary occasions — no special meaning | For sad occasions — condolences

履物　　Footgear

Zōri and *geta* are the well-loved traditional footgear of Japan. They both have a Y-shaped thong which is gripped between the big toe and the second toe and passes over the top of the foot.

For men ↙

For women ↘

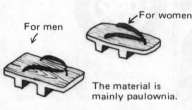

The material is mainly paulownia.

Geta. Wooden sandals with high supports. *Geta* are either carved in one piece, or the supports are inset into the foot-piece.

Underneath

Setta. A leather sole is fixed to the underneath with metal fastenings.

Ashida, or *takageta, geta* with very high supports for rainy days.

Pokkuri for women

Zōri. The sole is covered with leather or cloth. *Zōri* are worn mainly by women with *kimono.*

Waraji. Woven straw sandals, hardly ever seen nowadays.

紋	Crest

Mon is the family crest possessed by every Japanese family. It is designed in black and white.

One sees *mon* on the crested formal *kimono* called *mon-tsuki*, on the *noren* (entrance curtain) at shops, or on *chōchin* (paper lanterns); or as the symbols of shrines and temples.

Noren
(See p.93)

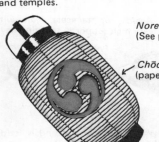

Chōchin
(paper lantern)

Kiri (paulownia):
Kiri and *kiku* (chrysanthemum) are used for the Imperial Family crest.

There are a great number of different *mon*, including such designs as plants, birds, characters, etc.

The *aoi*, or hollyhock, was the crest of the *Tokugawa-shōgun* family, which reigned over Japan from the 17th through the 19th centuries.

This *mon* has Mt. Fuji and a sailboat in a circle. Mountains are used for *mon* as well. *Takeda Shingen,* a *samurai* in the *sengoku* (Warring States) era, used one of them for the design on his banner.

A *mon* whose design is a Chinese character.

Yama-ni-kasumi: a mist hanging over a mountain.

The *tsuru,* or crane, is a lucky bird in Japan. It often appears in Japanese folk tales.

Chō: (butterfly)

Fundō: (balance)

Ise-ebi-maru: (lobster)

色と柄 | Color & Patterns

Traditional Japanese designs can be seen on *kimono* and *yukata* (see p. 56), and on *tenugui* (hand towels), *furoshiki* (wrapping cloths) and *chiyogami*.

Hanten, or short coat, with *asa-no-ha* (hemp leaf) pattern.

The *tenugui*, or hand towel , is not merely used for wiping hands and face; in olden times it was also a stylish accessory to one's costume.

Furoshiki with *kara-kusa moyō* (arabes-que) pattern.

Sakura, or cherry blossoms

Ichimatsu moyō, or chequered design

Nami, or wave

Uroko, or scales

Chiyogami (patterned paper) with various Japanese designs

A doll made of Japanese paper

The designs shown in the figure below have long been regarded as symbols of good luck and are still widely used.

Shō-Chiku-Bai

Shō or *Matsu*   *Chiku* or *Také*   *Bai* or *Umé*

Because the *Shō* (pine), *Chiku* (bamboo) and *Bai* (plum) are hardy plants that do well in the cold, they were regarded as symbols of good fortune.

Tsuru-Kamé

Tsuru or crane   *Kamé* or turtle

Cranes which are said to live for 1000 years and turtles which are said to live for 10,000 years are symbols of longevity.

Celebratory occasions in Japan are indicated by the colors red and white, while occasions of mourning are indicated by black and white.

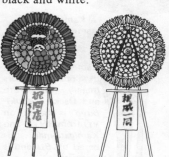

Cloths with broad red-and-white stripes are used on happy occasions, while ones with black-and-white stripes are used on sad occasions.

A *hanawa* is a large, circular floral decoration made with artificial flowers, sent and received on occasions of celebration such as the opening of a new shop or restaurant, and on sad occasions such as funerals. The size and number of the *hanawa* indicate the power and influence of the sender and receiver.

舞踊　Classic Dance

Buyō, Japanese dances, were developed based on incantations such as invocations of the spirits of the dead and prayers for the repose of souls. *Buyō* consists of the following three elements:

- *Mai* (舞) means to turn the body round.
- *Odori* (踊) means to jump.
- *Furi* (振) means to impersonate movements reflecting everyday and social conditions.

Mai, *odori*, and *furi* are described in their original meanings above, but they all mean dancing now.

Buyō was refined in *Noh, Kyōgen* and *Kabuki* drama. Dances in *Kabuki* were mainly developed in Tōkyō in the 19th century and *Nihon-buyō* and *Kabuki-buyō* are almost synonymous.

A *Kamigata-mai* named "Snow fall"

Kamigata-mai was developed at parlors mainly in Kyōto and Ōsaka. *Kabuki-buyō* is based on YŌ from *BUYŌ* and *Kamigata-mai* is based on *BU* and is more static.

Fujimusumé, or wistaria girl, is one of the more famous dances. A girl, as beautiful as a wistaria nymph, dances with all her love for a man in a background of wistaria.

短歌・俳句 Tanka & Haiku

Tanka is a type of short poem with lines of five, seven, five, seven and seven syllables, unique to Japan. The *tanka* is regarded as one of Japan's principal literary forms and has been read through the ages. The card game *hyakunin isshu* (see p. 132) is also an anthology of *tanka*.

Haiku are shorter than *tanka*, having lines of five, seven and five syllables. In *haiku*, the poet attempts to express his deepest emotions by describing nature in simple but beautiful language.

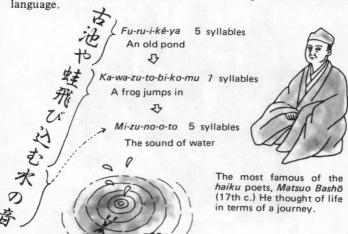

古池や蛙飛び込む水の音

Fu-ru-i-ké-ya   5 syllables
An old pond

⇩

Ka-wa-zu-to-bi-ko-mu   7 syllables
A frog jumps in

⇩

Mi-zu-no-o-to   5 syllables
The sound of water

The most famous of the *haiku* poets, *Matsuo Bashō* (17th c.) He thought of life in terms of a journey.

This famous *haiku* of Bashō's has occupied the minds of countless commentators throughout the ages. The interpretation of *haiku* is extremely difficult, but one of the pleasures of studying them lies in pondering the meaning that lies behind the words.

禅・座禅　Zen & Zazen

Zazen is a form of mental or spiritual training which originated in India. When doing *Zazen*, the practitioner sits with the correct posture, breathes regularly, and abandons worldly thoughts. *Zazen* was introduced to Japan from China, and a sect was established which used the method to achieve spiritual enlightenment.

Meditation (performing *zazen*) performed twice a day, early in the morning and in the evening.

Kyōsaku, a stick made of oak, used to hit trainees on the shoulder when their attention wanders.

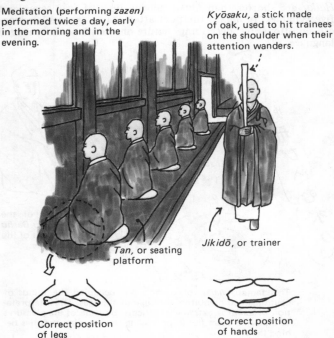

Tan, or seating platform

Jikidō, or trainer

Correct position of legs

Correct position of hands

The doctrine of *zen buddhism* can be described as wordless communication, or expression without language. It is a basic tenet of *zen* that the truth can only be attained through direct experience. Various training methods including *zazen* are employed to achieve this end.

Bamboo hat

Metal bowl (The priest is neither pleased when he is given something, nor disappointed when he is not).

Bell

Jōgu-bodai, Geké-shujō. These words state the basic purpose of *zen*, that is, to practice *zen* meditation in the search for *Bodai* (*Satori*, or spiritual enlightenment), while praying for the salvation of all living things including oneself.

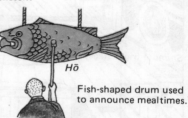

Hō

Fish-shaped drum used to announce mealtimes.

A priest performs no productive labor, but lives by begging food and money. This is called *takuhatsu*, and is a method of effacing oneself and becoming free of vanity.

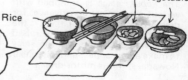

Miso soup   Pickles   Boiled vegetables

Rice

A typical dinner (one bowl of soup and two vegetable dishes, plus rice).

歌舞伎　Kabuki

Kabuki is one of Japan's traditional stage arts along with *Noh*, *Kyōgen* and *Bunraku*. It is said to have originated in the seventeenth century when it was first performed by the female dancer *Izumo-no-Okuni* and her troupe in Kyōto.

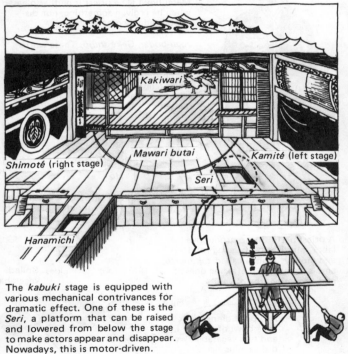

Kakiwari

Mawari butai

Shimoté (right stage)

Kamité (left stage)

Seri

Hanamichi

The *kabuki* stage is equipped with various mechanical contrivances for dramatic effect. One of these is the *Seri*, a platform that can be raised and lowered from below the stage to make actors appear and disappear. Nowadays, this is motor-driven.

Kabuki is characterized by its stylized acting, its gorgeous costumes and its spectacular scale. However, the features which spring most readily to mind in connection with *kabuki* are probably the *mawari-butai*, or revolving stage, the violent makeup of the *aragoto* actor, and the *oyama*, or female roles, played by male actors.

Mawari-butai: A revolving stage used to shift scenes.

Hanamichi: An aisle stage running from the stage to the rear of the theater through the audience.

Kakiwari: Painted scenery and props.

Kuroko is a kind of stagehand who sometimes appears on the stage to help the actors but has no direct connection with the story. By convention, he is treated as invisible by the audience.

Chanting or *shamisen* music is performed on this upper stage, called the *degatari-dai*, which revolves and carries the performers away and out of sight when they have finished.

Oyama: Some of most beautiful sights in *kabuki* are provided by the costumes and make up of the *oyama*, or female roles.
In early times, women who were also prostitutes played female roles, but this was prohibited during the *Tokugawa* shogunate on the grounds that it would harm public morals. Since then, female roles have been performed by male actors, with the unexpected result that the beauty of *oyama* has been produced.

Kabuki

The origin of the word *Kabuki* is "*Kabuku*" (incline), which has the additional connotation of strange actions, styles, etc. When it originated, *kabuki* was popular among common people, since *kabuki* directly and boldly expressed their dreams and emotions.

Ōdachi, a broadsword more than two meters long

Gohon-kuruma-bin, a wig with appendages like crabs' legs

Niō-dasuki, a decorative rope

> *Aragoto*: *Aragoto* is a style of acting for expressing anger. A hero who was tragically sent to the next world becomes a supernatural being and returns to this world for revenge.

Ōsuō, made from layers of hemp

A typical *Aragoto*, figure (from *Shibaraku*)

Red makeup is used for heroes, and black for villains.

Kumadori:
Makeup is applied with greasepaint, following the muscles of the face.

Kabuki as performed in modern times was refined during the 18th and 19th centuries. Before that period, *kabuki* involved simple erotic dances, acrobatics and short plays, but it was raised to the status of a serious theatrical art by the writer *Chikamatsu Monzaemon* (1653 – 1724) and the actor *Ichikawa Danjūrō*.

Kabuki has its own special movements and acting conventions. The words describing these have extended their meanings and are used as part of everyday conversation.

Janomé-gasa, an oiled-paper umbrella with a bamboo framework, decorated with a bull's-eye design.

Hachimaki, or headband

Wakizashi, or short sword

Sukeroku, a typical *Nimaimé* figure.

Glossary

● *Mié (-o-kiru).* In order to make his appearance even more impressive, the *kabuki* actor exaggerates his gestures and pauses, holding the pose at the critical point.

● *Nimaimé.* The role of a young, good-looking beau. Comic roles are called *Sanmaimé.*

● *Keren (-mi).* A technique by which the actor shows that he is concealing his true intentions, making him look wily or crafty.

● *Jūhachiban.* The eighteen best *kabuki* plays. Also used to mean a party trick or special talent.

● *Tachimawari.* A fight scene, played in a very stylized fashion , similar to dancing.

This was the most chic and fashionable style of the period.

Information

Kabuki-za: Take the Ginza subway line and get off at Ginza station.
Tel. (03)541-3131   Time: 11:00 ~ /17:00 ~
Admission: ¥1,500 — ¥15,000

能・狂言　Noh & Kyōgen

Noh is the oldest of Japan's theatrical arts. It is a comprehensive art form, embodying not only music, dance and literary art, but also sculpture, dyeing and weaving, and construction arts.

The distinctive feature of *noh* is its restraint, in contrast to *kabuki*'s extrovert liveliness. It is this feature of *noh* which has led to it being likened to 'moving sculpture'.

Agemaku (Curtain)

Jiutaiza (Chorus area)

Wakishōmen (Side seating)

Honbutai (Main stage)　*Shōmen* (Front seating)

The noh stage

All the actors in *noh* are male, and women's parts are played by men. The main protagonist is called *shité*, and the supporting actors are called *waki*. The *shité* cover their faces with special masks.

MASKS

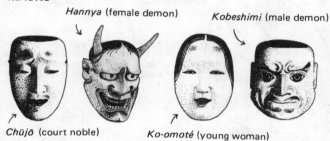

Hannya (female demon)

Kobeshimi (male demon)

Chūjō (court noble)

Ko-omoté (young woman)

The only props used in *noh* are small and simple, since *noh* relies heavily on symbolism for its effect.

TSUKURIMONO (PROPS)

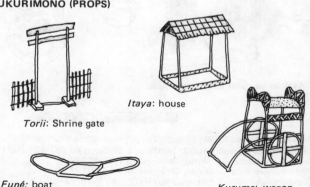

Torii: Shrine gate

Itaya: house

Funé: boat

Kuruma: wagon

Kyōgen is the traditional comedy of Japan. It has its own tradition separate from *noh*, but is often classed together with *noh* since it is used to fill in the interludes of a long *noh* drama and afford light relief.

A fan can be used skillfully in various ways to represent a dagger, a saw, a spear, a plate, etc.

Kyōgen is usually performed without masks, but occasionally the masks shown here are used. The emphasis in *kyōgen* is on humour.

Kyōgen contains a lot of dialogue.

← Nohkan

Main noh theatres:

Kokuritsu-gekijō-nohgakudō: Sendagaya, Shibuya-ku (03)423-1331
Kanze-nohgakudō: Shōtō, Shibuya-ku (03) 469-5241
Ginza-nohgakudō: Ginza, Chūō-ku (03) 571-0197
Kongō-nohgakudō: Nakagyō-ku, Kyōto-shi (075)221-3049

文楽 　　Bunraku

Bunraku is the traditional Japanese puppet theater, in which puppets are skilfully manipulated to act out a narrative (called *jōruri*) recited to the accompaniment of the *shamisen.

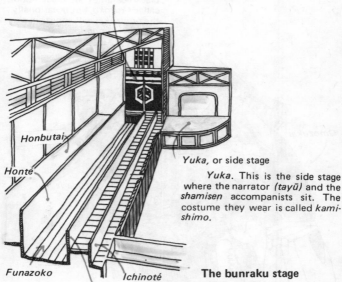

Agemaku (entrance curtain)

Honbutai

Honté

Funazoko

Ninoté

Ichinoté

Yuka, or side stage

Yuka. This is the side stage where the narrator *(tayū)* and the *shamisen* accompanists sit. The costume they wear is called *kamishimo*.

The bunraku stage

The puppeteers usually stand on the lowered parts of the stage called *honbutai* or *funazoko* and hold the puppets so that their feet are over the *honté* or the *ninoté*.

---

* Shamisen: See page 54.

There are usually three puppeteers for each puppet. One is responsible for the expression on the puppet's face and for its right arm and hand, and is called *omozukai*. The next operates the puppet's left arm and hand, and any props it is carrying, and is called *hidarizukai;* and the third moves the puppet's legs and is called *ashizukai*.

The puppeteers normally wear black costumes and black hoods, called *kuroko,* but occasionally the *omozukai* will appear in a hoodless *kimono*.

Omozukai

Hidarizukai

Ashizukai

To become an accomplished *omozukai* has been said to take a total of thirty years; ten years as *ashizukai,* a further ten years as *hidarizukai,* and ten years as *omozukai*.

* *Kuroko:* See page 69.

The puppets consist of a head *(kashira)*, shoulder-pieces *(kata-ita)*, a trunk *(dō)*, and legs and arms *(te-ashi)*. Various mechanisms operate to give the puppet an extremely lifelike appearance on the stage.

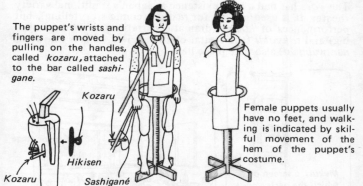

The puppet's wrists and fingers are moved by pulling on the handles, called *kozaru*, attached to the bar called *sashigane*.

Kozaru

Kozaru

Hikisen

Sashigané

Dōgushi

Female puppets usually have no feet, and walking is indicated by skilful movement of the hem of the puppet's costume.

The main internal part of the puppet's body is called *dōgushi*. The *hikisen,* or cord, inside this moves the puppet's head, and the small *kozaru* handles move its eyes, mouth, and eyebrows.

Keisei
(Prostitute)

There are various puppet heads for roles of different sex, age, character, etc; and the way the hair is arranged can show the character's position in life.

Wakaotoko
(Boy)

Gabu

The face of a beautiful woman can be made to change suddenly into the face of a demon.

寄席 Variety Theater

The *yose* has had a long existence as Japan's traditional variety theater. It is used mainly for *rakugo* (comic storytelling), but performances of *kōdan* (dramatic narration), *kijutsu* (conjuring) and *rōkyoku* (the recital of the ancient ballads known as *naniwabushi*) also take place here.

Mekuri, a screen on which the performer's name is displayed.

Kōza, or stage

Variety Theater

A performance of *kōdan* at *Tōkyō Honmokutei* theater. This is the only *tatami*-matted theater left in Tōkyō.

Kōdan. The art of reciting historical episodes with special intonation. The only props used are a low desk, called *shakudai,* and a stick called *Hariōgi.*

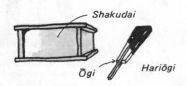

Shakudai

Ōgi

Hariōgi

Ōiri-bukuro. When there is a particularly large audience, the performer receives a bonus which is placed in this envelope.

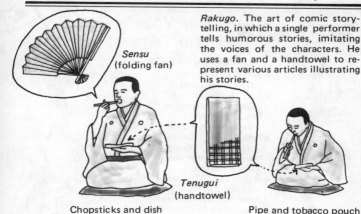

Rakugo. The art of comic story-telling, in which a single performer tells humorous stories, imitating the voices of the characters. He uses a fan and a handtowel to represent various articles illustrating his stories.

Sensu
(folding fan)

Tenugui
(handtowel)

Chopsticks and dish

Pipe and tobacco pouch

Manzai. This has enjoyed a boom among young people in the last few years. It consists of a comic dialogue, as opposed to *rakugo*, in which there is only one performer.

Kyokugei (juggling)

Information

Honmoku-tei : Ueno, Taitō-ku (03) 831-6137
Suehiro-tei : Shinjuku, Shinjuku-ku (03) 351-2974
Suzumoto-engei-jō : Ueno, Taitō-ku (03) 834-5906

正月・年中行事 New Year's Day & Other Annual Events

ANNUAL EVENTS

- Jan. 1st *(Shōgatsu)*
  New Year's Day
- Jan. 15 *(Seijin-no-hi)*
  Coming-of-Age-Day
- Feb. 3 *(Setsubun)*
  Bean-Throwing Ceremony
- Feb. 11 *(Kenkoku-kinembi)*
  National Founding Day
- March 3 *(Hina-matsuri)*
  Girl's Festival
- March 20 *(Shumbun-no-hi)*
  Vernal Equinox Day
- April 8 *(Hana matsuri)*
  Buddha's Birthday Festival
- April 29 *(Tennō-tanjōbi)*
  The Emperor's Birthday
- May 3 *(Kempō-kinembi)*
  Constitution Memorial Day
- May 5 *(Kodomo-no-hi)*
  Children's Day or Boys' Festival
- July 7 *(Tanabata)*
  The Star Festival
- Mid September *(Tsukimi)*
  Moon Viewing
- September 15 *(Keirō-no-hi)*
  Respect-for-the-Aged-Day
- September 23 *(Shūbun-no-hi)*
  Autumnal Equinox Day
- October 10 *(Taiiku-no-hi)*
  Health-Sports Day
- November 3 *(Bunka-no-hi)*
  Culture Day
- November 15 *(Shichi-go-san)*
  Festival day for children of 3, 5 and 7 years of age
- November 23 *(Kinrō-kansha-no-hi)*
  Labor Thanksgiving Day
- December 31 *(Ō-misoka)*
  New Year's Eve

80

● = National holiday

正月 **Shōgatsu**

There are more traditional decorations, games and customs associated with New Year *(Shōgatsu)* than with any of the other holidays or festivals on the Japanese calendar.

Shimenawa: The special twisted straw rope called *shimenawa* is put over the door of a house to bring good luck to the house and keep evil out.

Kadomatsu: This decoration, made from pine branches, bamboo and straw, is used in pairs, one on each side of the front gate or door or a house. The pine tree is a symbol of longevity.

Shimekazari: The crops of the harvest are offered to the gods in thanks and to pray for good harvests in the coming year. The prawn is also a symbol of a prayer for longevity.

Kagamimochi: This is also an offering to the gods. It consists of two *mochi*, or rice cakes, one on top of the other, and is placed in the *tokonoma*, or alcove of the main room of the house.

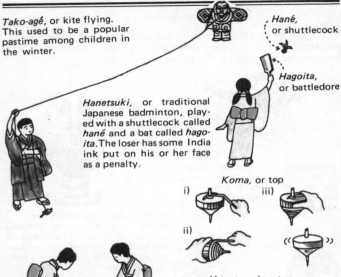

Tako-agé, or kite flying. This used to be a popular pastime among children in the winter.

Hané, or shuttlecock

Hagoita, or battledore

Hanetsuki, or traditional Japanese badminton, played with a shuttlecock called *hané* and a bat called *hagoita*. The loser has some India ink put on his or her face as a penalty.

Koma, or top

i)

ii)

iii)

Karuta, or card games. The one played especially at New Year is *Hyakunin-Isshu*, the Verses of a Hundred Poets. (see p.132)

How to spin a top.
i) Attach the cord to the upper spindle.
ii) Wind the cord round the lower spindle
iii) Throw the top and spin it by pulling the cord.

Fukuwarai: In this game, the player is blindfolded and has to draw in the eyes, nose and mouth on a girl's face drawn on a piece of paper. The girl's face is usually the *okame* face of *kagura*. (see page 23)

Shishimai: In this ceremony to drive out evil spirits, the performer puts on a head and cloak to become a lion and dances from house to house. Recently this custom has become a rare sight in cities.

Hatsumōdé: During the period from *joya-no-kané,* on New Year's Eve, until 7th January, people pay their first visit of the year to a shrine or temple to pray for health and happiness in the coming year. This is called *hatsumōdé.*

Otoshidama: This is the name for pocket money given to children by parents and relatives at New Year.

Grasp the bell-rope in the right hand and ring the bell.   Bow twice   Clap the hands twice   Bow once more

Correct method of praying

Ichinojū (top tier)   *Ninojū* (second tier)

Osechi: Osechi, or *Osechi-ryōri,* is a special kind of cooking for New Year. It is prepared in a four-tiered lacquered box called *Jūbako.*

Sannojū (third tier)   *Yonojū* (bottom tier)

節分 **Setsubun**

Setsubun (Feb. 3). This festival takes place on the day before *Risshun*, the first day of spring on the Chinese calendar. Roasted soybeans are scattered in and around the house to drive out sickness and misfortune, represented by a demon. (this custom is called *mamé-maki*.)

These days, *sumō* wrestlers and other well-known personalities are often invited to perform the bean-throwing ceremony at shrines and temples.

ひな祭り **Hinamatsuri**

Bonbori, a floor lamp made of Japanese paper over a bamboo frame.

Hinamatsuri (March 3). Dolls wearing traditional *kimono* are displayed to pray for the happiness of girls. These dolls are called *hinaningyō*, and the custom is also known as *momo no sekku*. In some areas, the old custom of loading one's troubles onto a paper doll and floating them off down the river is still practised. This is called *nagashi-bina*.

花見 **Hanami**

The cherry blossom, or *sakura*, is the national flower of Japan and is the favorite of most Japanese. From March to April, parties known as *hanami* (flower viewing) are held in the open air under the blossoms.

Ueno Park, one of the best-known parks in Tōkyō.

Yaé-zakura

Somei-yoshino

Goza (mat)

彼岸 **Higan**

Higan: This is the seven-day period whose middle day is *shunbun-no-hi* (the vernal equinox) *or shūbun-no-hi* (the autumnal equinox). During *ohigan*, people visit the graves of their ancestors to pray for the souls of the deceased.

An (sweet bean jam)

Mochigomé (sticky rice)

Ohagi: *Ohagi* is a special kind of rice cake coated with sweet bean jam that is put as an offering on Buddhist altars during *ohigan*.

Yōji

Hakamairi (a visit to a grave to pray)

Sotōba

Senkō (incense)

Water is sprinkled over the grave to purify it.

子供の日 **Kodomo-no-hi**

Kodomo-no-hi (May 5). Also called *tango-no-sekku*, this is a festival for children and a national holiday. Families with boys put up *koinobori*, or carp streamers, in their garden and a display of dolls called *gogatsu ningyō* in a room of the house.

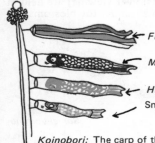

Fukinagashi (pennant)

Magoi (a black carp, representing the father of the house)

Higoi (a red carp, for the mother)

Smaller carp, one for each son

Koinobori: The carp of the *koinobori* appear to be swimming vigorously against the current. Boys should face and overcome their difficulties with the same positive spirit.

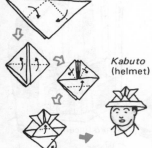

Kabuto (helmet)

How to fold paper to make a helmet

Gogatsu ningyō: The dolls are usually placed on a stepped dais with three levels. There is a set of *samurai* armour, *a taiko,* or big drum, and the other things needed to fight an old-style battle.

七夕 **Tanabata**

Tanabata (July 7). This is the one day of the year on which, according to ancient Chinese legend, the Weaver Princess (Vega) and the Cowherd (Altair) can cross the Milky Way that separates them and renew their love for each other.

Bamboo

Tanzaku: This is a special strip of paper on which poems are written. *Tanzaku* and other ornaments are hung on a bamboo branch during *tanabata* and placed in the garden as a way of praying for better things to come.

月見 **Tsukimi**

Tsukimi (Mid - Sept.). *Tsukimi,* or 'moon-viewing' takes place at full moon in autumn, which is known as *Jūgoya.* A spot is chosen from which to admire the moon, and decorations of *tsukimidango* (rice dumplings), *susuki* (pampas grass) and autumn fruit are displayed.

Susuki

Tsukimi dango

Nana-kusa
(the Seven Autumn Flowers)

七五三 **Shichi-go-san**

Shichi-go-san (Nov. 15). At *shichi-go-san*, people dress their children up in *kimono* or their best clothes and take them to a local shrine to pray for their health and happiness. This is done with girls and boys of three years old, boys of five, and girls of seven.

These paper bags contain red and white stick-shaped sweets (*Chitose-amé*) which are said to confer a thousand years' happiness on the children who receive them.

クリスマス **Christmas**

Everybody is aware of Christmas in Japan, not only members of the Christian church; but there is no special holiday from work for Christmas, and it is treated rather like St. Valentine's Day, as a commercial affair.

Christmas cakes are sold and eaten on Christmas Eve

大晦日 **Ōmisoka**

Kiné, or pestle →

Mochi, or pounded glutinous rice.

Usu, or mortar

At the end of the year, rice is pounded for the special rice cakes known as *mochi*. The pounding of the rice is called *mochitsuki*.

Noshi, a strip of dried abalone wrapped in red and white paper and used to decorate a gift

Mizuhiki; red and white cords used for tying gifts

Seibo: This is the name of the gift-giving season at the end of the year, when people send presents to all those from whom they have received favors. There are two such seasons in the year, the other, called *Chūgen*, being in the middle of July.

Joya-no-kané means the ringing of the temple bell one hundred and eight times at temples all over the country at midnight on New Year's Eve.

Toshikoshi soba: Toshikoshi means 'seeing out the old year and seeing in the new' and *toshikoshi soba* is *soba*, or buckwheat noodles. They are eaten on New Year's Eve, because the long thin noodles symbolize longevity.

---

* *Joya-no-kané:* See page 29.

祭り	Festival

Japan was originally a country of farmers, and most of its festivals are connected with the agricultural calendar. Every region has its own Autumn festival to thank the local deity for the harvest and to pray for an even better one next year.

The *Mikoshi* is a portable *Shintō* shrine which is taken out and paraded through the streets of the town during festivals. The spirit of the local deity is said to come down and reside in the *mikoshi* during these proceedings.

The local people carry the *mikoshi* on their shoulders. The clothes they wear for this were originally modelled on the costume of a fire-man, or *Tobi* of the *Edo* era.

Hōō, or Chinese phoenix

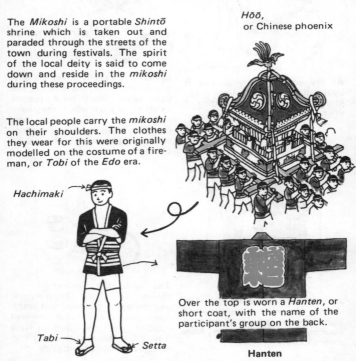

Hachimaki

Tabi   Setta

Over the top is worn a *Hanten*, or short coat, with the name of the participant's group on the back.

Hanten

Dashi

The *Dashi* is a festival float with wheels, decorated with flowers and dolls. It is paraded through the streets in the same way as *mikoshi*, and the local deity is believed to descend to the *Hoko*, or decorative halberd, on the top of the float.

The *Namahagé* of *Akita* is a demon who chastises lazy people. He is not considered an evil demon, but one who brings happiness.

Hanagasa-matsuri: This festival is held on August 6 and 7 in Yamagata City. It is highlighted by a gala parade of people carrying umbrellas with flowers on top.

During festivals, people dress up as deities and give various performances designed to appease the gods and induce them to grant a good harvest, or to drive away evil spirits.

Festival

The *Nebuta* festival takes place from August 2nd to 7th in *Aomori*. In it the *Nebuta*, a figure made of decorated paper stretched over a framework of bamboo, wood and wire with a lantern inside it, is paraded through the city amid crowds of people. *Nebuta* represents the god of sleep, equivalent to the Greek god Morpheus.

In the *Kantō* festival in *Akita*, which takes place from August 4th to 7th, forty-six lanterns are mounted on a bamboo pole about ten meters long.

Aomori

Akita • Sendai

Kyōto

Nagasaki

The **Tanabata* festival in Sendai is from August 6th to 8th.

The *Gion* festival in Kyōto is the festival of the *Yasaka* Shrine. It lasts about one month, from July 1st to 30th, and during it, on July 17th, decorated floats called *Yama* and *Hoko* are paraded through the city.

Okunchi festival takes place from October 7th to 9th in *Nagasaki*.

92

*Tanabata: See page 87.

のれん	Noren

Noren are the half-curtains hung over the entrances of Japanese restaurants and other establishments. They act as a sign for the establishment and carry the name or type of store, or the service provided. They were originally used as sunshades.

Noren are made of cloth and are generally navy blue with white letters. They can be seen at traditional Japanese restaurants, public baths *(Sentō)*, grocery stores or traditional Japanese fan makers *(Ōgiya)*.

Nawa noren (noren made of cords) are used at the entrances of the traditional drinking-houses called *Ippai nomiya.*
Today *nawa noren* and *ippai nomiya* have become synonymous.

縁日・市　Festival Day & Market

An *en-nichi*, or festival day, is a day connected with Shintoist and Buddhist deities. Visitors to shrines and temples on this day can receive special divine favors. On *en-nichi*, shrine and temple grounds are alive with people, and street stalls do a thriving business.

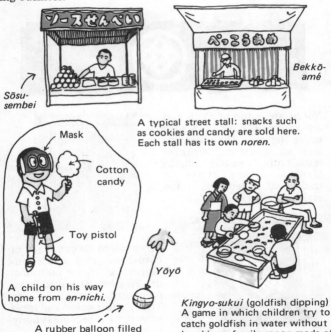

Sōsu-sembei

Bekkō-amé

A typical street stall: snacks such as cookies and candy are sold here. Each stall has its own *noren*.

Mask

Cotton candy

Toy pistol

A child on his way home from *en-nichi*.

Yōyō

A rubber balloon filled with air and water.

Kingyo-sukui (goldfish dipping) A game in which children try to catch goldfish in water without breaking a fragile spoon made of thin paper.

Asagao-ichi, or morning glory fair, is held at *Iriya,* Tōkyō every July. All kinds of morning glory are display-ed and sold at street stalls.

Hagoita --- →

Hagoita-ichi, or old-fashioned Japanese battledore fair, is held at *Sensō-ji* Temple in Tōkyō on the 17th, 18th and 19th of December.

Tori-no-ichi, lit. the cock fair, is a fair at which *kumadé,* or decorative bamboo rakes, are sold. It is held at *Ōtori* Shrine in Tōkyō on *Tori-no-hi* in November, which is the day for the 10th zodiac sign, a cock.

Jindaiji-daruma-ichi, a *daruma* doll fair at *Jindaiji* Temple.

Hōzuki-ichi, a Chinese lantern plant fair, is held at *Sensō-ji* Temple.

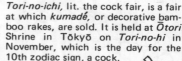

Rotenshō, street-stall keepers and showmen, give performances and sell things to crowds on days like *en-nichi,* for their living. They have their own associations.

盆踊り　Festival Folk Dance

Bon is one of Japan's summer festivals and is a time when people make offerings of food and other things to their ancestors and pray for the happiness of their ancestors' souls in the next world. It takes place from the 13th to the 15th of August, and during this time the folk dance known as *Bon Odori* can be seen in cities, towns and villages all over Japan.

Yagura

Chōchin, or lantern

A *Taiko*, or large drum, is set up on the stage and played to set the rhythm.

Uchiwa, or non-folding fan

Yukata, an informal cotton *kimono*

The usual practice is for a stage called *Yagura* to be set up in the town or village and for everybody to dance around it in a big circle. Sometimes, however, people dance in procession through the streets, and this is called *Nagashi*. (Awa Odori)

Awaodori. This is a free kind of dancing style practised in the Tokushima pref. of Shikoku. It is often likened to the carnival of Rio de Janeiro. During the daytime a rather quiet and restrained dance called *Nagashi* takes place, while at night, a much more lively dance called *Zomeki* can be seen.

Sugegasa, or sedge hat

Udenuki, or armlet

Tenugui, or hand towel

Kedashi, or decorative underskirt

Shirotabi, or white *tabi*.

Hiyorigeta, or low, dry-weather *geta.*

Yukata

Famous *bon odori* dances:
Kankō Odori (Ise)
Daimoku Odori (Kyōto)
Kisobushi (Nagano)

As part of the *Bon* festival, a bonfire called *Mukaebi* is lit, at the beginning, to welcome the souls of the ancestors back to Earth, and another called *Okuribi*, at the end, to send them off. In Kyōto, on 16th August, a huge fire in the shape of the Chinese character *dai* (大 , meaning 'big') is lit on Mt. Nyoigataké. This is called *Daimonjiyaki*.

十二支　　Jūni-shi

Jūnishi is the twelve signs of the oriental Zodiac. They are related to the date, the time of day, and the compass directions.

The *Jūnishi* is not used as a calendar in Japan today, but everybody knows the animal representing the year in which he or she was born. When the sign of a particular year is the same as a man's birth sign, he is termed *toshi-otoko*, while a woman is termed *toshi-onna*.

Animal and Year

	1936	1948	1960	1972	1984
NE (Rat)	1936	1948	1960	1972	1984
USHI (Ox)	37	49	61	73	85
TORA (Tiger)	38	50	62	74	86
U (Hare)	39	51	63	75	87
TATSU (Dragon)	40	52	64	76	88
MI (Serpent)	41	53	65	77	89
UMA (Horse)	42	54	66	78	90
HITSUJI (Sheep)	43	55	67	79	91
SARU (Monkey)	44	56	68	80	92
TORI (Cock)	45	57	69	81	93
INU (Dog)	46	58	70	82	94
I (Boar)	47	59	71	83	95

The *Jūnishi* (12 animal signs) can be seen on the *Ema*(See page 22) and on stamps.

鬼門 North-East and South-West, termed *kimon* and *urakimon* respectively, are considered unfavourable directions likely to bring bad luck.

七福神 | Shichifuku-Jin

The *Shichifukujin*, or the Seven Deities of Good Fortune, include six gods and a goddess, and they come from various sources such as Shintoism, Buddhism, Taoism, Brahmanism, etc.

Daikoku, the god of wealth, wears a hood and holds a big bag filled with treasures on his left shoulder and an *uchide-no-kozuchi* (a lucky mallet) in his right hand. (See page 102)

Ebisu, the god of fishermen, holds a big red *tai*, or sea bream, under his left arm and a fishing rod in his right hand.

Fukurokuju and *Jurōjin* (the aged gods of wealth and longevity) inhabit the same body, that of a long-headed old man. He holds a cane with a *makimono* (scroll) tied around it, and an *ōgi* (folding fan).

Kisshōten

A second goddess called *Kisshōten* is sometimes included among the *Shichifukujin*.

Hotei, the god of contentment and happiness, holds a big bag and an *ōgi* (a fan). He is said to be the only human being among the *Shichifukujin*.

Bishamon, the god of warriors, wears armor and carries a small pagoda.

Benten, the goddess of eloquence, music and wisdom, plays the *biwa* (Japanese mandolin).

The *Shichifukujin* are said to enter port on a *takarabuné* (a ship laden with treasure) on New Year's Eve to bring happiness to everybody. Pictures and *takarabuné* decorations are one of the ornaments used at New Year for good luck.

縁起物 Good Luck Talisman

Engimono are thought to bring good luck and are sold mainly at shops within shrine grounds. People buy them in the hope of having better fortune, harvests, hauls of fish, or business.

The *maneki-neko*, or beckoning cat, is thought to bring good business and is a decoration for shops.

This paw calls in customers and money.

When the Japanese want to make a wish come true, they often buy a *Daruma* doll and paint in one of the eyes. If the wish does in fact come true, they paint in the other eye as a sign of gratitude. Election candidates always have one of these dolls in their campaign office.

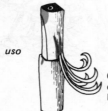

uso

Old dolls are exchanged for new ones at shrines to pray for good luck in the New Year.

This carved wooden doll is shaped like an 鷽 *uso* (a bullfinch). Another Chinese character with the same reading, 嘘 *uso* (a lie) represents sin and unhappiness, and these two characters are punned and the bullfinch is treated as embodying the sins of the previous year. The sins are expurgated when the doll is exchanged for a new one at New Year.

Uchide-no-kozuchi, a small golden mallet, symbolizes wealth and prosperity. It is said that one can attain anything one wishes if one shakes it.

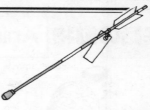

Kumadé, or decorative bamboo rakes, are said to rake up good fortune and are sold at *tori-no-ichi*. (See page 95.)

Hamaya, an arrow with the power of exorcising evil spirits, is bought by people visiting shrines at New Year to pray for happiness.

Inu-hariko, or papier-mâché dog, is a charm to help women in childbirth and in raising their children.

Shichifukujin, the Seven Deities of Good Fortune, (See page 101) are on *takarabuné,* a ship laden with treasure.

Akabeko, a red papier-mâché cow or ox, is a charm to keep away misfortune.

Wara-uma, a straw horse, is a charm for a good harvest.

103

民話の動物 Animals in Fables

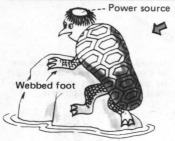

Power source

Webbed foot

Kappa is a kind of water sprite that lives in rivers. It has a characteristic hair style called *okappa atama*, and has a plate filled with water on top of its head. It is said that the *kappa* will lose its power if it does not have this water. The *kappa* is a mischievous creature and sometimes plays tricks like pulling horses into the river.

Tiger skin loincloth

Ryū (Tatsu); a dragon, looks like a gigantic snake, flies all over the sky, and breathes fire. A dragon symbolizes evil in western countries, but in Japan it is the god of clouds and rain and is one of the twelve signs of the zodiac.

Kaminari, the god of thunder, straddles clouds wearing a loincloth made of tiger skin, pounding on a drum. Japanese parents often warn their children that *kaminari* will steal their belly-buttons if they stick them out too far.

Horns

Oni, a sort of goblin, eats human beings, has horns on its forehead and fangs in its mouth and wears a loincloth on its naked body. In Japan, *oni* is a familiar figure in folk tales such as *Momotarō*, the hero who went to beat up *Oni*, accompanied by a pheasant, monkey and dog. *Oni* shows up in many tales.

Long nose

Wings

Tengu, a kind of goblin who lives in the mountains, looks like a human being but has a long nose and two wings, so it can fly all over the sky. Saying *tengu-ni-naru*. (becoming *tengu*) means to be boastful about your own exploits and ability.

Kitsuné, a fox, is a real animal but is considered supernatural in Japan. *Kitsuné* is the object of worship of *Inari Shinkō*, an old folk religion.

105

占い　Fortune-Telling

There are many different methods of fortune-telling practised in Japan, but the most popular are astrology, palm-reading and *ninsō uranai*, which is physiognomy, or fortune-telling from a study of a person's facial and other features. You can see *ekisha*, or fortune-tellers, on any busy street at night, sitting behind a small table in the open air, with just a candle lantern to cast a dim light.

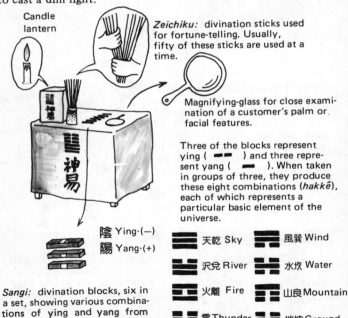

Candle lantern

Zeichiku: divination sticks used for fortune-telling. Usually, fifty of these sticks are used at a time.

Magnifying-glass for close examination of a customer's palm or facial features.

Three of the blocks represent ying (▬▬) and three represent yang (▬). When taken in groups of three, they produce these eight combinations (*hakkē*), each of which represents a particular basic element of the universe.

陰 Ying·(—)
陽 Yang·(+)

Sangi: divination blocks, six in a set, showing various combinations of ying and yang from which the customer's fortune is told.

天乾 Sky　　　風巽 Wind

沢兌 River　　水坎 Water

火離 Fire　　　山艮 Mountain

雷 Thunder　　地坤 Ground

106

Palm-reading and physiognomy are not uncommon in the West, but they are usually used to divine a person's character or abilities, while in the East they are used mainly to predict a person's fate.

Tesō-uranai (palm-reading)

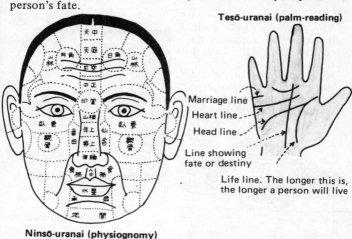

Marriage line

Heart line

Head line

Line showing fate or destiny

Life line. The longer this is, the longer a person will live

Ninsō-uranai (physiognomy)

Other types of fortune-telling

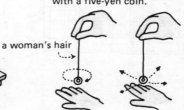

Predicting the sex of a baby with a five-yen coin.

Cloudy

Rain

Fair

a woman's hair

Geta-uranai: a method of predicting the weather. A *geta*, or wooden sandal, is kicked into the air and the weather is forecast by the way it falls.

The baby will be a girl.

The baby will be a boy

銭湯　Public Bath

The *sentō*, or public bath, is where the Japanese go to have their daily bath if they do not have a bathroom at home. In the old days, it also used to serve as a meeting-place for the exchange of gossip.

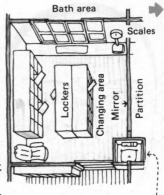

Bath area

Scales

Lockers

Changing area

Mirror

Partition

Bandai: (Attendant)

湯

男　Men

女　Women

Entrance

Recently, the number of public baths has decreased.

When you duck under the curtain at the main entrance of the *sentō*, you will see two entrances, one for men and one for women.

Take your shoes off and put them in one of the lockers provided, then go in the appropriate entrance and pay the attendant, who sits in a high box overlooking the men's and women's changing areas. Take your clothes off in the changing area and enter the bath area, not forgetting your soap, facecloth, etc. You can leave your clothes in one of the lockers.

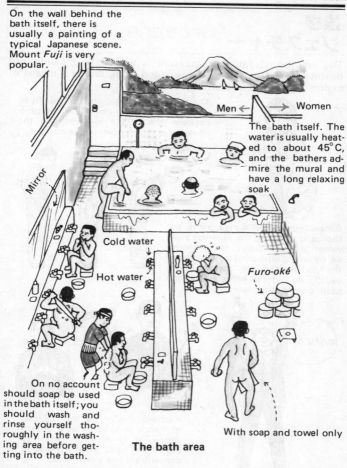

On the wall behind the bath itself, there is usually a painting of a typical Japanese scene. Mount *Fuji* is very popular.

Men ← → Women

The bath itself. The water is usually heated to about 45°C, and the bathers admire the mural and have a long relaxing soak

Mirror

Cold water

Hot water

Furo-oké

On no account should soap be used in the bath itself; you should wash and rinse yourself thoroughly in the washing area before getting into the bath.

The bath area

With soap and towel only

挨拶・ジェスチャー　Greeting & Gesture

The traditional Japanese greeting is not shaking hands, but bowing from the waist. This is called *Ojigi*, and is a means of expressing respect and affection.

The degree of inclination, from slight to very low, depends on the relationship between the people involved and the situation in which bows are exchanged.

Banzai, whose literal meaning is 'ten thousand years', is the Japanese equivalent of 'three cheers'. It is performed by raising both arms straight above the head and shouting *'Banzai'*, and is usually done three times at the high point or end of a celebration.

BANZAI

Kashiwadé refers to the clapping of hands in worship at a *Shintō* shrine. It is done in order to attract the gods' attention and to concentrate one's own mind.

Tejimé stems from *kashiwadé*. In it, the hands are clapped a total of ten times in a 3-3-3-1 rhythm. This is called *ippon-jimé*, and three sets of it is called *sanbon-jimé*.

Tejimé is performed at the end of celebrations or meetings to bring things to a lively close.

SHAN SHAN SHAN!

Gestures often used by the Japanese:

Waving a hand this way means "come here."

OIDE, OIDE

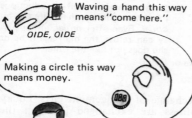

Making a circle this way means money.

首

Kubi (fired)

The gesture of pretending to cut off the head means "to be fired."

Two people join little fingers like this when they make a solemn promise.

Let's drink *saké*.

My girl friend

ME?

Counting gesture:

1 2 3 4 5

Indicating number:

1 2 3 4 5

結婚式 | Wedding Ceremony

In addition to *ren-ai* marriages (marriages in which couples meet spontaneously and marry for love) there are matched marriages, called *omiai* in Japan. In matching couples, particular emphasis is placed on hobbies and the educational background and the social status of both families. A person who arranges this meeting, as a go-between, is called *nakōdo*.

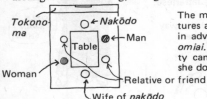

The man and woman exchange pictures and written self-introductions in advance before they agree to an *omiai*. Even after *omiai*, either party can refuse the marriage if he or she does not like the other.

Yuinō is the ceremonial exchange of engagement gifts. Lucky objects symbolizing happiness are exchanged between the families of the betrothed.

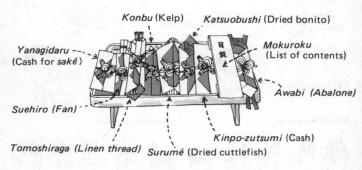

A set of nine lucky objects for yuinō:

There are three kinds of wedding ceremony; *Shintō*, Buddhist and Christian. The type of ceremony and the couple's own religion are not always the same.

Uchikaké:
A long overgarment for *kimono*.

Tsuno-kakushi, lit. a cover for horns, is a kind of veil which is said to hide the bride's horns of jealousy.

A *Shintō* priest takes charge of the purification, the wedding vows and the exchange of rings.

Montsuki & Hakama (See P. 57)

San-san-kudo is a ceremony in which cups of *saké* are exchanged as a wedding vow. The ceremony starts with a small cup and finishes with a large cup.

chōshi

sanbō

three times three

San-san-kudo

The wedding reception is usually held after the ceremony.

At the reception desk, those attending sign their names and give a special envelope called *shūgi-bukuro*, with money in it, as a wedding present.

Shūgi-bukuro is tied with gold and silver paper strings which are impossible to untie, symbolizing a wedding that will last for ever.

The bride changes her clothes two or three times during the reception. This practice is called *oiro-naoshi.*

The most popular order for changing clothes is: *Uchikaké* (a long overgarment for *kimono*) → *Furi-sodé* (*kimono* with long sleeves) → a western style dress.

Lately, many grooms change their clothes as well.

Nakōdo

Cutting the wedding cake is one of the main events at the reception.

The seating order of those attending depends on their age, social status and the closeness of the relationship between them and the married couple. The closer to the main table, the more important the seat.
The parents of the married couple sit at the back of the reception hall.

じゃんけん　Jan-ken

This is the simplest possible game for establishing a winner and a loser, and it is the first game that Japanese children learn. No equipment is required to play it. It takes no time at all, and you can see it being played all over Japan at all times of the day and night. Where people in Western countries would toss a coin, the Japanese play *Janken*.

Jan-Ken-Pon!

The two players shout *"jan ken pon!"*, and simultaneously form their hands into shapes representing a stone (*Gū*), scissors (*Choki*) or paper (*Pā*). The winner is decided according to the diagram.

Win　　　　　Lose

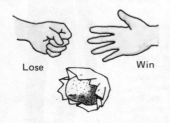

Lose　　　　　Win

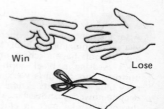

Win　　　　　Lose

SCISSORS, PAPER, STONE

Elementary school pupil

Japanese children start elementary school at the age of seven and attend for six years. Most schools have no school uniform, but recently, some are making it compulsory for pupils to wear yellow hats or helmets for traffic safety.

Name tag

Satchel for schoolbooks, etc.

Sērā-fuku
(Sailor suit)

Junior high school pupil

Tsumé-eri

School uniform
Black or navy-blue

Leather briefcase

After elementary school, there are three years of junior high school. Most junior high schools have a school uniform, the boys wearing a black military-looking uniform and the girls wearing black or navy-blue sailor suits. These are on the decline nowadays, however. After school, the pupils take part in club or sports activities.

High school students and the Examination Hell

After junior high school, there are three years of senior high school. Senior high school students are forced to cram hard for their university entrance examinations, and parents spare no trouble or expense to help their offspring get into the best university they can.

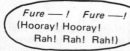

Fure — !   Fure —!
(Hooray! Hooray!
   Rah! Rah! Rah!)

University student

University undergraduate courses last four years, and students specialise in a particular choice of subject. However, most students do not study very hard but simply enjoy university life. When one university competes against another at sports, the old-style supporters' groups can still be seen, but the Western influence has appeared recently with the increasing number of cheer girls.

サラリーマン	# Salaryman

The word *salaryman*, coined in Japan, refers to all white-collar company employees, usually those engaged in desk work in private companies. These are the men who have brought about Japan's stunning economic growth.

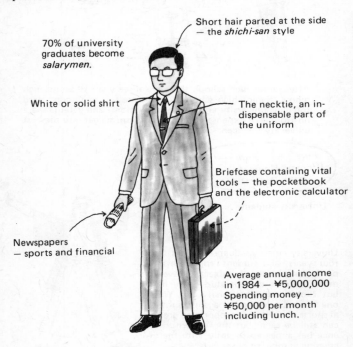

70% of university graduates become *salarymen*.

White or solid shirt

Short hair parted at the side — the *shichi-san* style

The necktie, an indispensable part of the uniform

Briefcase containing vital tools — the pocketbook and the electronic calculator

Newspapers — sports and financial

Average annual income in 1984 — ¥5,000,000 Spending money — ¥50,000 per month including lunch.

Mr. Average *Salaryman*

A Salaryman's Survival Kit

Meishi, or name card. This establishes the *salaryman*'s identity. Name cards are exchanged without fail when meeting someone for the first time.

Hanko, or personal seal (See page 120.)

Electronic calculator. Mass-produced at low prices, these have become one of the things people associate most closely with Japan.

Bank cards and credit cards

Writing instruments

Pocket cassette recorder with English tape. *Salarymen* who can not speak English are considered to have an insufficiently international outlook.

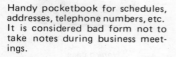

Handy pocketbook for schedules, addresses, telephone numbers, etc. It is considered bad form not to take notes during business meetings.

Salaryman's data bank — from trade journal to pinup magazine.

はんこ　Personal Seal

In Japan the *hanko*, or personal seal, has all the legal validity that a signature has in other countries, while a handwritten signature is not recognized in law. Both companies or other organizations and individuals possess *hanko*, and every adult Japanese will have two or three, one of which is officially registered and is called *jitsuin*.

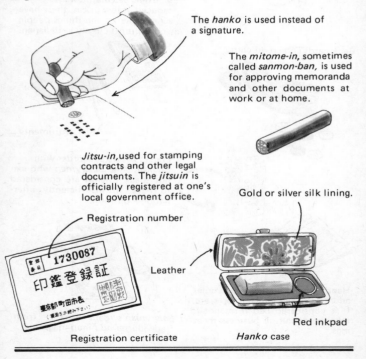

The *hanko* is used instead of a signature.

The *mitome-in*, sometimes called *sanmon-ban*, is used for approving memoranda and other documents at work or at home.

Jitsu-in, used for stamping contracts and other legal documents. The *jitsuin* is officially registered at one's local government office.

Gold or silver silk lining.

Registration number

1730087

印鑑登録証

東京都町田市長

（裏面もお読み下さい）

Leather

Red inkpad

Registration certificate

Hanko case

巡査・交番 Policeman & Police Box

Japan is said to be the safest country in the world because of its low crime rate. You can see the *kōban*, or police box, in every town and village and scattered throughout the city. The policemen in the police box, fondly known as *omawarisan*, are not only there to fight crime. They also help people with directions and recovering lost property.

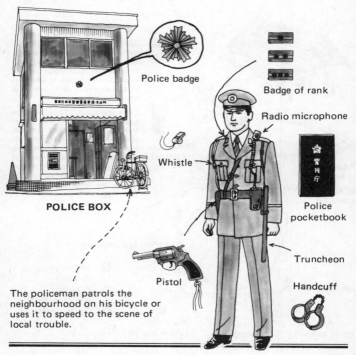

Police badge

Badge of rank

Radio microphone

Whistle

POLICE BOX

Police pocketbook

Pistol

Truncheon

Handcuff

The policeman patrols the neighbourhood on his bicycle or uses it to speed to the scene of local trouble.

大相撲 | Ō-zumō

Sumō, or Japanese wrestling, is a national sport that ranks in popularity with baseball. It is a professional sport, and the unique combination of ancient ceremony and the tremendous power of the wrestlers themselves makes it a marvellous and exciting spectacle.

Kokugikan. (The *sumō* stadium.)

Seating capacity: 11,098
Site area: 35,700 sq.m.
Floor area: 12,400 sq.m.

Shioiré, or salt container. Before each bout, the wrestlers scatter salt in the ring to purify it. About thirty kilograms of salt is used in this way every day during a tournament.

Chikaramizu. This is the special name for the water the *sumō* wrestlers refresh themselves with before each bout. The winner of the previous bout and one of the wrestlers from the following bout serve it in ladles to the wrestlers in the ring.

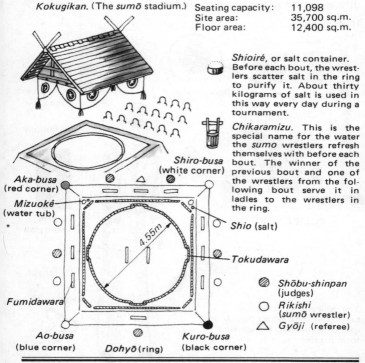

Shiro-busa (white corner)

Aka-busa (red corner)

Mizuoké (water tub)

Shio (salt)

4.55m

Tokudawara

Fumidawara

⊘ *Shōbu-shinpan* (judges)

○ *Rikishi* (*sumō* wrestler)

△ *Gyōji* (referee)

Ao-busa (blue corner)

Dohyō (ring)

Kuro-busa (black corner)

Explanation of wrestlers' actions

Magé, or topknot

Mawashi, or belt

Sagari, or apron

Sonkyo. This squatting posture was a way of showing respect to one's betters in the olden days.

Shiko. When the wrestlers raise their legs high and stamp them down onto the ring, they are symbolically crushing any evil spirits that may still be lurking there.

Chirichōzu, or *chiri.* When the wrestlers clap their hands twice and spread out their arms with their palms visible, they are showing that they are carrying no concealed weapons.

Shikiri

This is when the wrestlers squat down on their marks and glare at each other, trying to 'psych each other out'. This action is repeated along with stamping and scattering salt.

Basic rules: the winner is the one who first makes his opponent step outside the ring or touch the ground (in or out of the ring) with any part of his body except the soles of the feet.

Main winning tricks

Yorikiri   Oshidashi   Uwatenagé

123

SUMŌ CEREMONIES

Tsuyuharai, or herald, who precedes the *yokozuna* into the ring.

The *gyōji,* or referee

Tachimochi

The *tsuyuharai* and *tachimochi* who accompany a *yokozuna* when he performs *dohyō-iri* are usually *makuuchi* wrestlers from the same *heya,* or stable, as the *yokozuna.*

The *yokozuna,* or grand champion

Keshō-mawashi, or ceremonial apron

Dohyōiri. In this ceremony, which takes place before each tournament begins, the *yokozuna* enter the ring one by one, accompanied by their herald *(tsuyuharai)* and swordbearer *(tachimochi)* and give a special performance with actions peculiar to *sumō.*

Yumitori, or bow dance. This ceremony is performed at the end of a tournament after all the matches are over. It is done to purify the ring, and is usually carried out by a wrestler from the *makushita* division or lower.

SUMŌ RANKING

横綱	Yokozuna
大関	Ōzeki
関脇	Sekiwaké
小結	Komusubi
前頭	Maegashira
十両	Jūryō

A wrestler is promoted if he wins eight or more of the fifteen bouts that make up one tournament. This record of wins is called *kachikoshi*. Eight or more losses is called *makekoshi*.

Sumō wrestlers all belong to training stables called *heya*, and a wrestler never fights another from the same *heya*.

Yokozuna is the highest rank a wrestler can achieve, and even if he records a *makekoshi* (eight or more losses) in a tournament, he cannot be demoted. However, *yokozuna* always retire as soon as their performance starts to become unworthy of their rank.
Ōzeki wrestlers are demoted if they record two successive *makekoshi*.

Gunbai

Gyōji (referee)

On the day before, the *Yobidashi* (announcers) walk through the neighborhood, beating the *fure-daiko* (a drum) to advertise the *Basho*.

Information

Jan. (New Year Tournament); May (Summer Tournament); September (Autumn Tournament) — *Kokugikan Sumō Stadium*
March (Spring Tournament) — *Ōsaka Furitsu Taiikukan*
July (Nagoya Tournament) — *Aichi Kenritsu Taiikukan*
Nov. (Kyūshū Tournament) — *Fukuoka Kokusai Center*

武道 | Martial Arts

JŪDŌ

Jūdō is known all over the world today, and the foundations of its development were laid in 1882 when *Jigorō Kanō* established the *Kōdōkan Dōjō*. The basic principle of *Jūdō* is 'strength with softness'. It is a sport which trains both the body and the mind, and it is Japan's best-known sport.

(A)

払腰 *Harai-goshi*

(B)

上四方固 *Kamishihō-gatamé*

Basic techniques

A) *Tachiwaza*, or standing techniques. Throwing the opponent from a standing position.

B) *Osaekomiwaza*, or *Newaza*. Holding the opponent down on the mat.

C) *Kansetsuwaza*. Getting a hold on one of the opponent's joints

(C)

腕挫十字固 *Udehishigi-jūji-gatamē*

Ippon!

In competition, a bout is won by throwing the opponent or getting a hold on him using one of the above techniques.

KARATÉ

Karaté was originally thought to have been developed as a means of attack and defence by the people of Okinawa, who at one time were forbidden to carry weapons. It is generally considered to be extremely aggressive, but the famous *karate* master *Gichin Funakoshi* taught the maxim that 'there is no first strike in *karaté*'.

(Front stance)
Zenkutsu

(Back stance)
Kōkutsu

Middle level front punch
Chūdan zuki

Sword hand block
Shutō-uké

Side kick
Yoko-geri

When two or more people practice *karaté* together, this is called *kumité*, or sparring, while when one person practices with an imaginary opponent, it is called *kata* (formal exercises).

A *kata* in which the movements of attack and defence flow and blend into one another.

127

KENDŌ

Kendō is the oldest of the martial arts. It embodies the swordsmanship practiced by the *samurai* together with their philosophy of life. Today it is a popular sport, practiced with bamboo swords and protective clothing, for the purpose of training mind and body.

Tsuba, or hilt

Shinai, a bamboo sword

MENN.....N !

Men, or mask

Koté, or arm protector

Dō, or chest protector

Taré, or protective apron

Kendō equipment

The winner wins by striking the opponent's mask (*men*), arm (*koté*) or body (*dō*) with the correct combination of force (both physical and spiritual), bodily posture, and sword position.

AIKIDŌ

Aikidō was originated by *Morihei Ueshiba*. It places great stress on the spiritual aspect and has been called '*zen* in motion' (see p. 66).

Aikidō, while a martial art, is not merely a matter of technique. It also teaches correct breathing and meditation, and is a way of 'encountering the energy of the universe'.

Aikidō movements are similar to those of *Buyō*, or classical Japanese dance.
Ki, or 'life force' emanates from the practitioner's finger-tips.

The opponent is thrown when the spirit manifests itself as physical power.

Shihō-nagé, one of the basic techniques.

子供の遊び Children's Games

Children's games soon go out of fashion, and the games shown here are not often seen these days. However, adults grow nostalgic when they talk about them.

Menko

Menko are thick cards with pictures on them. One player lays his card on the ground, and the other player tries to turn it over by slapping his own card down on top of it. If he succeeds, he keeps the first player's card.

win! lose

Bīdama

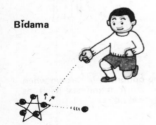

Kendama

Bīdama or marbles are colored glass balls, the same as in Western countries. The rules are similar to billiards.

Otedama

Otedama is a kind of juggling game in which a child tosses up and catches two or more cloth bags containing *azuki* beans, usually singing a song at the same time

Origami

In *origami,* square pieces of paper are artfully folded to make animals, dolls, boats, etc., without using scissors or paste.

Crane

Ayatori

Ayatori is the Japanese version of cat's cradle. String is twined around the fingers to make various shapes and patterns. A child can play by himself, or two can play, taking turns.

Can be stretched like rubber

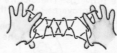

4-step ladder

Koma

(Spinning top)

Hanetsuki

(similar to badminton)

Koma and *Hanetsuki*: See page 82.

Japan has its own versions of the West's playing cards and Tarot cards. Three of the most popular kinds are *Irohagaruta*, *Hanafuda* and *Hyakunin-isshu*.

● **Irohagaruta**

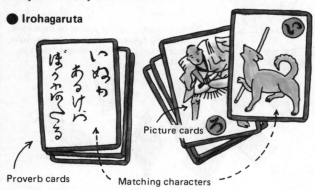

Proverb cards

Matching characters

Picture cards

Irohagaruta consists of two sets of forty-eight cards. The first set is printed with forty-eight proverbs or sayings, each beginning with a different letter of the Japanese alphabet, and the second set has pictures representing the proverbs. The picture cards are spread out and the referee reads out the proverbs, while the players search for the matching picture card.

The referee reads the proverbs.

Dumpling (=Pudding) rather than Cherry-blossoms (=praise)

The players try to find the matching picture card.

● Hyakunin-isshu

The cards in *hyakunin-isshu* are each printed with a different poem by one of a hundred well-known traditional poets. The game is played in a similar way to *Irohagaruta*.

● Hanafuda

In *Hanafuda*, there are forty-eight cards, each with a particular flower representing one of the twelve months of the year. Like twenty-one or poker, it is a good game for gambling.

January (pine) — February (plum) — March (cherry) — April (wisteria) — May (iris) — June (peony)

July (bush clover) — August (eulalia) — September (chrysanthemum) — October (maple) — November (willow) — December (paulownia)

パチンコ　Pachinko

A *Pachinko* machine is a kind of vertical pinball table. It is a cheap form of gambling that anybody can enjoy and is extremely popular. It is played individually.

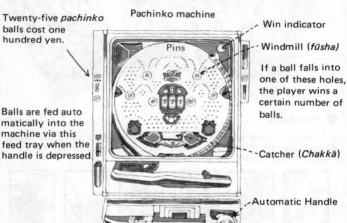

Pachinko machine

Twenty-five *pachinko* balls cost one hundred yen.

Pins

Win indicator

Windmill (*fūsha*)

If a ball falls into one of these holes, the player wins a certain number of balls.

Balls are fed automatically into the machine via this feed tray when the handle is depressed

Catcher (*Chakkā*)

Automatic Handle

Ash tray

Pachinko parlour

On the latest throttle-type machines, if three sevens appear in a row, the catcher at the bottom will open up ten times, for thirty seconds a time.

After playing, a player can exchange his or her *pachinko* balls for cigarettes, biscuits and other prizes. The exchange counters in some *pachinko* parlours are beginning to look more and more like supermarkets.

134

麻雀　Mahjong

Mahjong, originally a Chinese game, was introduced into Japan from China and the United States at about the same time, in the 1920s. It is a game for four players, who draw and discard tiles (equivalent to playing cards) in turn until one of the players has completed his hand by grouping his tiles into certain prescribed combinations.

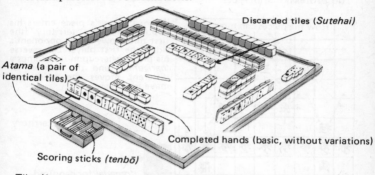

Discarded tiles (*Sutehai*)

Atama (a pair of identical tiles)

Completed hands (basic, without variations)

Scoring sticks *(tenbō)*

Tiles (four of each variety, thirty-four varieties; total 136 tiles)

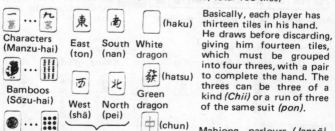

一萬 ··· 九萬
Characters
(Manzu-hai)

東
East
(ton)

南
South
(nan)

□ (haku)
White
dragon

🀐 ··· 🀘
Bamboos
(Sōzu-hai)

西
West
(shā)

北
North
(pei)

發 (hatsu)
Green
dragon

🀡 ··· 🀙
Circles
(Pinzu-hai)

Winds
(kaze-hai)

中 (chun)
Red
dragon

Basically, each player has thirteen tiles in his hand. He draws before discarding, giving him fourteen tiles, which must be grouped into four threes, with a pair to complete the hand. The threes can be three of a kind *(Chii)* or a run of three of the same suit *(pon)*.

Mahjong parlours *(Jansō)* can be found in cities and towns all over the country.

135

将棋　Shōgi

Shōgi is similar to Western chess in that the player who first checkmates his opponent's king is the winner. There are no queens but there are "*kin*"(gold) and "*gin*"(silver) pieces. However, there is a big difference; in *shōgi*, a player can use his opponent's captured pieces as his own. Now, there are about 100 professional players.

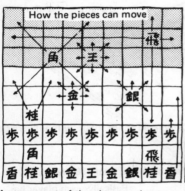

How the pieces can move

When a player's piece enters his opponent's home territory (the first three rows on the opponent's side), the first player can reverse his piece, whereupon it becomes a *'narigoma'*, and the number of different moves the piece can make is increased.

▨ = Opponent's territory

Komadai: for captured pieces not yet being used by the player who captured them.

Arrangement of the pieces at the start

King	Rook	Bishop			Knight		Pawn
Ōshō	*Hisha*	*Kaku*	*Kin*	*Gin*	*Keima*	*Kyōsha*	*Fu*

Narigoma

囲碁　Igo

Go, or *igo*, is a game played by two players using round black and white stones respectively, who take turns to place their stones on a board marked off into nineteen lines by nineteen lines. The stones are placed not in the squares but on the intersections of the lines forming the squares, and the object is to capture more territory than one's opponent.

There is a handicapping system for when one player is better than the other. This is called *Teaiwari*.

Black (who plays first) has 181 stones. White has 180.

Goban

Goishi

(1)

(2)

(3)

Counting up territory. This is done by counting the total number of intersections enclosed by a player's stones. In the example shown, this is six.

Capturing stones. In example 1, 2, and 3 on the right, if White places his next stone in position 'a', then Black's stone is captured and is removed from the board.

日本文字　Japanese Letters

The Japanese language is a member of the Altaic family of languages, and it has many words in common with Korean and Chinese. However, its syntax is quite different from that of Chinese.

Japanese is written using Chinese characters in combination with two syllabaries named *hiragana* and *katakana.*.

The Chinese characters, or *kanji,* all have meanings, while *hiragana* and *katakana* represent sounds only. Here are a few examples:

- *Kanji* (Chinese characters)

Kanji are ideographs representing objects or ideas.

How some simple *kanji* representing objects developed:

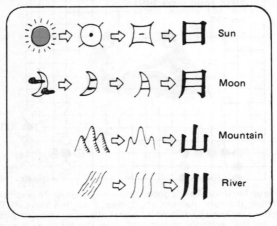

How *kanji* are combined to make words:

自 + 動 + 車 = 自動車

Automatic + movement + wheel = car

時 + 計 = 時計

Time + measurement = clock

- Characters representing concepts

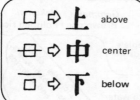

口 ⇨ **上** above

囲 ⇨ **中** center

口 ⇨ **下** below

- The *hiragana* sound syllabary was developed from the cursive writing of whole *kanji*

安 → 女 → あ ª
以 → 以 → い ⁱ
宇 → 宇 → う ᵘ
衣 → む → え ᵉ

- The *katakana* sound syllabary was developed from parts of *kanji*

阿 → β → ア ª
伊 → イ → イ ⁱ
宇 → ウ → ウ ᵘ
江 → エ → エ ᵉ

米・味噌・醬油 Rice, Miso & Soysauce

■ Rice (Komé)

The staple diet of the Japanese is rice, and since it is also the basic raw material of *miso* and vinegar, it is an indispensable part of Japanese life.

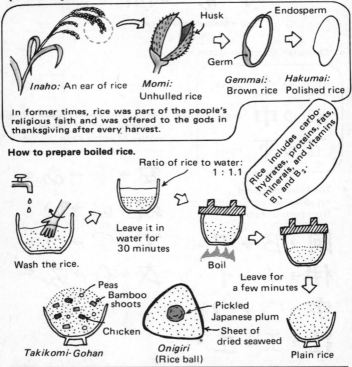

Inaho: An ear of rice

Momi: Unhulled rice

Husk
Endosperm
Germ

Gemmai: Brown rice

Hakumai: Polished rice

In former times, rice was part of the people's religious faith and was offered to the gods in thanksgiving after every harvest.

Rice includes carbohydrates, proteins, fats, minerals, and vitamins B_1 and B_2.

How to prepare boiled rice.

Wash the rice.

Ratio of rice to water: 1 : 1.1

Leave it in water for 30 minutes

Boil

Leave for a few minutes

Peas
Bamboo shoots
Chicken

Takikomi-Gohan

Pickled Japanese plum
Sheet of dried seaweed

Onigiri (Rice ball)

Plain rice

■ Miso and Soysauce (Shōyu)

Miso and soysauce are indispensable flavouring elements in Japanese cooking. They have recently become more popular in the West, but to the Japanese, they are not merely flavourings but an essential part of life.

● How to prepare miso-shiru

Niboshi, small dried sardines

Katsuobushi, dried bonito shavings

Tōfu

Japanese radish

Miso is made by fermenting steamed, salted soy beans, rice, wheat or other grains.

味噌

Yellowish brown paste

Shōyu was introduced to Japan from China. It is used as a basic element in almost all Japanese dishes.

KIKKOMAN Soy Sauce

Different kinds of soysauce container

刺身　Raw Fish

Sashimi, or raw seafood, including fish, shellfish, prawns, etc., is one of the typical foods of Japan, and is invariably served at any Japanese-style inn *(ryokan)* or restaurant. It is usually dipped in soy sauce before being eaten.

Ikizukuri consists of a whole fish, usually sea bream *(tai)* or carp *(koi)*, carefully sliced so as not to kill it, and arranged on a bed of garnishings so that it looks as if it is still in its natural state.

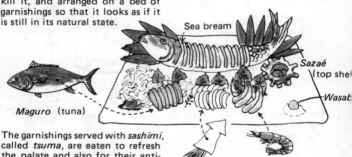

Sea bream

Sazaé (top shell)

Wasabi

Maguro (tuna)

The garnishings served with *sashimi*, called *tsuma*, are eaten to refresh the palate and also for their antiseptic properties. They include beefsteak plant leaves *(shiso-no-ha)*, Japanese radish *(daikon)*, cucumber *(kyūri)* and chives *(asatsuki)*.

Ika (squid)

Ebi (shrimp)

One essential accompaniment to *sashimi* and *sushi* is Japanese horseradish, or *wasabi*, a root which is grated to give a pale green, pungent condiment.

Katsuo

Tataki is chopped raw fish, usually bonito *(katsuo)* or horse mackerel *(aji)*.

Wasabi

Aji

142

寿司 Sushi

The *Edomaē* of *Edomaezushi* (also known as *nigirizushi*) refers to *Edo*, the old name of Tōkyō. *Maē* means 'in front of', and the name arose because the ingredients for *Edomaezushi* were caught in the bay in front of the city. The term *Edomaezushi* also refers to the unique atmosphere of a good *sushi* shop, lively and high-spirited.

When you sit at the counter, you can order what you want from the ingredients displayed in the glass case in front of you, and the chef will prepare your *sushi* as you order it.

The best way for beginners to order *sushi* is to have one of the sets with fixed prices, known as *matsu* or *tokujō* (extra special); *takê* or *jō* (special); and *umé* or *nami* (standard). *

Glass case   **Wooden counter**

Sushi shops have a special argot of their own; the bill, for example, is called *oaiso*, instead of the usual *kanjō*, and green tea is referred to as *agari* instead of *ocha*.

The art of cutting and arranging the bamboo and other leaves that decorate the *sushi* bowls is also part of the *sushi* chef's craft.

---

* *Matsu, take, ume*: See page 63.

Sushi

There are several different kinds of *sushi*, such as *Edomaezushi* (also called *nigirizushi*); *makizushi*, or roll *sushi*; and *hakozushi*, or pressed *sushi*. *Edomaezushi* is most popular in the *Kantō* area, while *hakozushi* prevails in the *Kansai* area. All types of *sushi* use rice seasoned lightly with vinegar.

Toro (Belly of Tuna)   *Maguro* (Tuna)

Ebi (Prawn)   *Tamago* (Egg)

Kohada (Punctatus)   *Anago* (Sea-eel)

Uni (Sea Urchin) *Ikura* (Salmon Roe)

To make *hakozushi*, the *sushi* rice with the *neta* on top is put in a rectangular wooden box and pressed, then taken out and cut into bite-sized pieces. Types of *neta* used include *anago* (conger eel), *kani* (crab) and *saba* (mackerel).

Hakozushi made with mackerel is called *battera*.

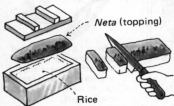

Neta (topping)

Rice

Nigirizushi consists of bite-sized amounts of *sushi* rice (*shari*) pressed into an oblong shape, with a piece of raw seafood, sweet egg omelette *(tamago-yaki)* or other food placed on top. The topping is called *neta*.

Wasabi (Japanese horseradish)

Shari (*sushi* rice)

Shōga or gari (ginger)

Neta (filling)

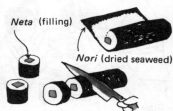

Nori (dried seaweed)

Makizushi is made by placing the *sushi* rice and the *neta* on top of a sheet of *nori* (dried seaweed) and rolling it into a cylinder. Various types of *neta* are used, such as cucumber, tuna, or *kampyō* (dried gourd).

天ぷら　　Tempura

Tempura consists of various kinds of fish, shellfish and vegetables coated in a light batter and deep-fried. It is a very popular meal, and the Japanese eat it at home or in speciality restaurants or other restaurants.

The batter, or *koromo*, is made from flour, egg yolks and water.

The ingredients are dipped in the batter.

The *tempura* is fried in vegetable oil.

Kisu, a small white fish

Nasu, or eggplant

Prawn

Shiitake, an edible fungus

Onion

Yakumi, or condiments

Tentsuyu, the broth into which you dip your *tempura*

Oshinko, Japanese pickles

A serving of *tempura*

すき焼・しゃぶしゃぶ　Sukiyaki & Shabu-shabu

Sukiyaki is a beef and vegetable dish which is cooked at the table. Thinly-sliced beef, vegetables, *tōfu*, etc., are boiled in a stock made from soy sauce, sweet rice wine and sugar. Sometimes the cooked ingredients are dipped in a mixture of raw egg before being eaten.

Edible chrysanthemum leaves

Shirataki, noodles made from devil's-tongue

Leeks

Tōfu

Beef

Raw egg

Iron cooking pot

Shabu-shabu, like *sukiyaki*, is based on beef and vegetables, but the meat is sliced paper-thin and is dipped briefly in boiling stock and then in a special sauce before being eaten. *Shabu-shabu* sauces are usually flavoured with *miso*, soy or sesame.

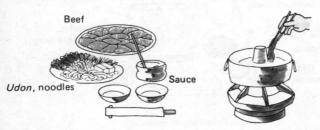

Beef

Udon, noodles

Sauce

炉端焼 Robata-yaki

Old Japanese houses used to have a square hearth, or *ro* in the center of one of their rooms, and the family would gather round this at mealtimes. The *robatayaki* restaurant is an attempt to recapture this homely atmosphere.

Fried *tōfu*

Ayu-no-shioyaki

Chicken

Charcoal grill

Sweetfish

Vegetables, etc.

Customers order their food and tell the chefs how they would like it cooked.

Chicken meatballs & baked mushrooms

Soba is a long thin brownish noodle made from buckwheat flour. There are various recipes using *soba* depending on the type of broth it is cooked in and the method of cooking. A serving of *soba* at a restaurant ranges from ¥400 to ¥800, making it an inexpensive dish.

Sobayu (The hot water from the boiled *soba*) — This is usually served with cold *soba* such as *mori soba*. After the *soba* is eaten, *sobayu* is added to the left-over sauce dip to make a bowl of soup to drink.

Tsuyu (Sauce dip)

Typical Japanese Soba — *Mori Soba*

In Japan, it is accepted practice to make a slurping sound when eating noodles.

Green peas

Egg

Koromo

Donburi

Pork

Steamed rice

A typical donburi dish is *katsudon;* Breaded deep fried pork cutlet served on top of rice.

Soba restaurants serve various kinds of *donburi* dishes besides *soba* dishes.

Udon is a noodle made of kneaded wheat flour, thicker than *soba* and whitish in color.

Shichimi
Seven spices including red pepper.

Aburaagé
Fried soybean curd nicknamed *Kitsuné* (fox).

Yakumi
Finely-chopped green onion used as a spicy condiment.

Kitsuné Udon is a typical *udon* dish.

Rāmen is a kind of Japanese-Chinese dish consisting of Chinese noodles served in a hot chicken broth made with soy sauce, *miso* (fermented soybean paste) or salt. *Rāmen* is one of the most popular dishes in Japan.

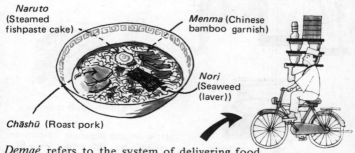

Naruto
(Steamed fishpaste cake)

Menma (Chinese bamboo garnish)

Nori
(Seaweed (laver))

Chāshū (Roast pork)

Demaé refers to the system of delivering food to your door. The delivery boys used to be like acrobats (as in the picture shown above) when delivering food, but now they use the back of motorbikes to carry the orders.

Demaé

うなぎ・どじょう Broiled Eels & Loaches

■ EELS

Eels are highly prized in Japan as a good food for building stamina. They are usually cooked in the form of *Kabayaki* by broiling them while basting them with a sauce made from eel stock, soy sauce, sweet rice wine and sugar, and are served on top of rice in a lacquer box.

Dressing the eel

Broiling over charcoal

Unajū: Broiled eels on top of rice in a lacquer box, with a special sauce.

It is an old Japanese custom to eat eels on *Doyō-no-ushi-no-hi* , about the 20th July, as a way of strengthening oneself against the enervating heat of midsummer. In the *Kansai* district, eels are called *mamushi,* which also means 'viper'.

150

Konazansho: Powdered *sansho*, or Japanese pepper, always sprinkled on *kabayaki* before they are eaten.

Kimosui: A clear soup containing the eel's liver.

These are served with *unajū*.

■ LOACHES

The best season for *dojō* (loaches) is from May to July, when they are cooked in the form of *tempura* or made into *Yanagawa-nabé*, a kind of hotpot with eggs, burdock root and soy sauce.

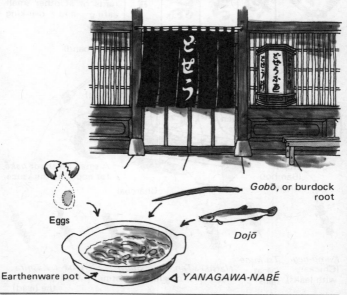

Eggs

Gobō, or burdock root

Dojō

Earthenware pot

◁ *YANAGAWA-NABÉ*

やきとり　　Yakitori

The original *yakitori* consisted of small pieces of chicken skewered on bamboo and cooked over a charcoal fire. Nowadays, most restaurants that sell this cheap and popular food also serve various parts of the pig and cow as well as the chicken. You can ask for *shio* (with salt) or *taré* (flavoured with a soy-based sauce).

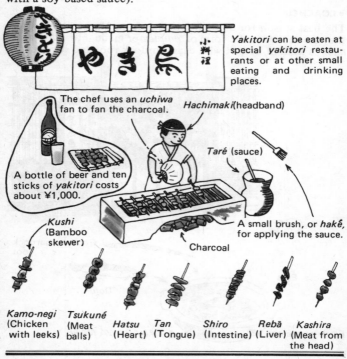

Yakitori can be eaten at special *yakitori* restaurants or at other small eating and drinking places.

The chef uses an *uchiwa* fan to fan the charcoal.

Hachimaki (headband)

Taré (sauce)

A bottle of beer and ten sticks of *yakitori* costs about ¥1,000.

A small brush, or *haké*, for applying the sauce.

Kushi (Bamboo skewer)

Charcoal

Kamo-negi (Chicken with leeks)　*Tsukuné* (Meat balls)　*Hatsu* (Heart)　*Tan* (Tongue)　*Shiro* (Intestine)　*Rebā* (Liver)　*Kashira* (Meat from the head)

おでん   Oden

Oden is the collective name given to various ingredients such as eggs, Japanese radish, fish cakes, *tōfu*, etc., cooked slowly in fish stock. People often cook it at home in the winter, or eat it as an accompaniment to beer and *saké*.

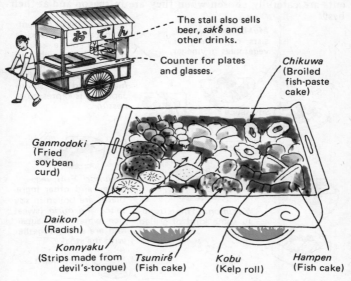

The stall also sells beer, *saké* and other drinks.

Counter for plates and glasses.

Chikuwa (Broiled fish-paste cake)

Ganmodoki (Fried soybean curd)

Daikon (Radish)

Konnyaku (Strips made from devil's-tongue)

Tsumiré (Fish cake)

Kobu (Kelp roll)

Hampen (Fish cake)

Oden can be eaten at small eating and drinking establishments, but it seems to taste even better when eaten at one of the many *yatai*, or street stalls, that move around the town at night. Try one of these if you want to sample a typical aspect of ordinary Japanese life.

会席料理 Kaiseki-ryōri

Kaiseki Ryōri is a style of cooking in which Japanese dishes are served to guests along with drinks at a dinner party. In Japan, there is a clear change in the climate from one season to the next, and this is reflected in *kaiseki ryōri*, since the ingredients are carefully chosen when they are in season and at their best.

Mukōzuké. This consists of *sashimi* or vegetables in vinegar.

Sakizuké

Soy-sauce

Hassun, This is so named because the food is arranged on a square tray measuring eight *sun* by eight *sun,* one *sun* being about three centimetres; and eight *sun* in Japanese is expressed as *hassun.*

Yakimono. This is usually some kind of grilled fish

Wanmori. Fish, vegetables and other ingredients are boiled in soy sauce and *mirin* (sweet rice wine) with sugar, and are served together with the stock.

Mushimono. A steamed dish containing egg, vegetables, fish, meat, etc.

Kōnomono

Miso shiru

Finally, rice *(meshi),* miso soup *(miso shiru)* and pickles *(Kōnomono)* are served to round off the meal.

As well as the *kaiseki ryōri* described here, there are two other types of formal Japanese meal, called *Honzen* and *Chakaiseki*. There are set rules for preparing, serving and eating these meals, and the trays used for serving them are sometimes also used for serving *kaiseki ryōri*.

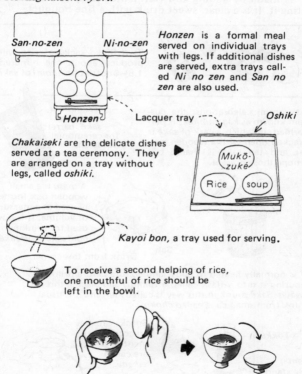

San-no-zen   *Ni-no-zen*

Honzen

Honzen is a formal meal served on individual trays with legs. If additional dishes are served, extra trays called *Ni no zen* and *San no zen* are also used.

Lacquer tray

Oshiki

Chakaiseki are the delicate dishes served at a tea ceremony. They are arranged on a tray without legs, called *oshiki*.

Mukō-zuké
Rice   soup

Kayoi bon, a tray used for serving.

To receive a second helping of rice, one mouthful of rice should be left in the bowl.

The proper method of removing the lid from a bowl.

酒　　Saké

Saké is made by adding *kōji* (fermented rice) to rice and fermenting it. It is a clear, sweet drink with a fine bouquet.

Two 60-kg sacks of rice will produce about one hundred 1.8–ℓ bottles (*isshōbin*) of saké

At special celebrations, the custom known as *kagamibiraki* is performed, in which a cask of *saké* is cracked open with a wooden mallet and the *saké* is shared out among those present.

Tsunodaru, a special *saké* barrel for ceremonial occasions.

A *masu* is a small wooden box formerly used as a measure of volume. It is now used for drinking cold *saké* (*hiyazaké*).

Salt

Drink from this corner.

Saké is normally heated to body temperature before drinking by pouring it into a flask called a *tokkuri* and placing this in hot water. *Saké* drunk in this way is called *kan*, and it is usually drunk from small cups called *choko*.

Tokkuri

Hakama, bottle stand.

Choko

Snacks eaten as an accompaniment to *saké* are called *sakana*.

Drink from this part.

和菓子 Confectionery

Japanese confectionery, or *wagashi*, is made mainly from rice or wheat flour, *azuki* beans, and agar-agar, a kind of gelatin made from seaweed. The various kinds of *wagashi* are associated with particular seasonal events on the Japanese calendar.

Sakuramochi: Sweet *azuki* bean paste in a rice cake, wrapped in cherry leaf pickled in brine. The leaf can also be eaten.

Kashiwamochi: Like *sakuramochi*, but wrapped in an oak leaf, usually eaten on Boys' Day, May 5th. You cannot eat the leaf of this one.

Monaka: A kind of wafer in the shape of a flower, filled with sweet bean jam.

Taiyaki: A very popular confection in the shape of a fish (the *tai*, or sea bream). The outside is a pancake made from flour, and the filling is sweet bean jam.

Senbei: Japanese-style crackers made from rice or wheat flour and flavoured with salt or soy sauce. Sometimes they are wrapped in *nori*, or dried seaweed.

Yōkan   *Shiruko*

Dango: Rice dumplings

Kuriyōkan: Sweet bean-paste jelly with chestnuts.

 ← *Manjū*

In most Japanese families, each of the family members has his or her own rice bowl and chopsticks. Children's training starts from the correct handling of chopsticks.

How to hold the upper chopstick. This one is held between the thumb and the index and middle fingers, and is moved up and down.

How to hold the lower chopstick. This one is kept still.

How to pick up a small object.

How to pick up a large object.

Do not stick your chopsticks straight up in your bowl of rice, as this is how a meal is offered on a Buddhist altar to the spirits of the dead.

Types of chopstick   *Waribashi*

Chopsticks should never be grasped in the fist in this way, since this is how they would be held for use as a weapon.

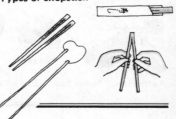

When setting a table, the rice bowl, chopsticks and soup bowl are always placed in the positions shown. Children are taught to distinguish left from right by telling them that their right hand is the one they hold their chopsticks in, while their left is the one that holds the rice bowl.

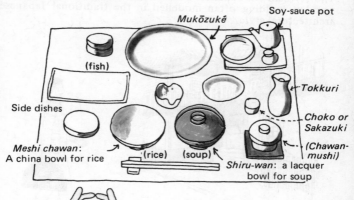

Mukōzuké

Soy-sauce pot

(fish)

Tokkuri

Side dishes

Choko or
Sakazuki

(Chawan-
mushi)

Meshi chawan:
A china bowl for rice

(rice)   (soup)

Shiru-wan: a lacquer
bowl for soup

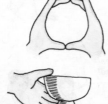

The diameter of rice and soup bowls used to be fixed at about 12 cm, the diameter of the circle made with the thumbs and middle fingers of both hands. However, women find this a bit too large, and most bowls for women have a diameter of about 11.4 cm.

Meotojawan refers to a pair of teacups made for husband and wife, the husband's being slightly larger than the wife's. This is not meant to imply that the husband is more important than the wife, but rather reflects the fact that the former is usually physically larger than the latter.

Meotojawan

日本旅館　Japanese Inn

The *Ryokan*, or Japanese inn, is usually a one- or two-storey wooden building often modelled in the traditional Japanese architectural style.

Entrance of a typical ryokan

Kimono-clad staff welcome guests with a smile at the entrance. Guests take off their street shoes and change into slippers here.

Irasshai-masé!

Change your shoes.

Instead of numbers, the guest rooms in a *ryokan* are named after Japanese flowers or plants, e.g. 'Chrysanthemum Suite', 'Cherry Suite', etc.

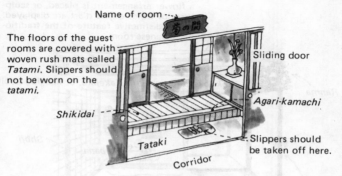

Name of room

The floors of the guest rooms are covered with woven rush mats called *Tatami*. Slippers should not be worn on the *tatami*.

Sliding door

Agari-kamachi

Shikidai

Tataki

Slippers should be taken off here.

Corridor

Entrance of guest room

After showing guests to their room, the maid will serve green tea and cakes, and bring the register for the guests to sign.

Zaisu

Green tea

Maid

Zabuton

In a *tatami* room, the seating consists of legless chairs (*Zaisu*) and cushions (*Zabuton*).

■ The interior of a ryokan

Tokonoma: The *tokonoma* is a recessed alcove in the wall where a scroll is hung, a flower arrangement is placed, or sculptures or other objets d'art are displayed. It is a distinctive feature of the traditional Japanese room.

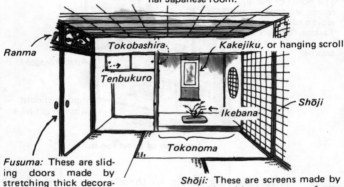

Ranma

Tokobashira

Tenbukuro

Kakejiku, or hanging scroll

Shōji

Ikebana

Tokonoma

Fusuma: These are sliding doors made by stretching thick decorative paper over both sides of a wooden frame.

Shōji: These are screens made by stretching thin paper over a frame of crossed laths, lighter than *fusuma* and allowing a diffused light to pass through.

Ranma: The *ranma* is a kind of openwork grating with various designs which allows light and air to pass through.

Maru-mado   *Katō-mado*   *Shitaji-mado*

Japanese-style window

The traditional Japanese sleeping arrangement is the *futon*, a kind of mattress with quilts that is spread out on the *tatami* for sleeping and put away during the day. In a *ryokan*, it is the maid's job to lay out the *futon* in the evening and put them away in the morning.

Makura, or pillow.

Oshi-iré: The *oshiire* is a kind of built-in cupboard where the *futon* and other household equipment are kept.

Mōfu, or blanket.

Kakebuton, or quilt.

Shikibuton, or mattress.

For keeping warm in the winter, there are the *Kotatsu* and the *Hibachi*.

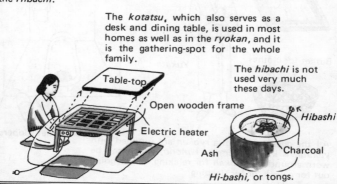

The *kotatsu*, which also serves as a desk and dining table, is used in most homes as well as in the *ryokan*, and it is the gathering-spot for the whole family.

The *hibachi* is not used very much these days.

Table-top

Open wooden frame

Electric heater

Hibashi

Ash

Charcoal

Hi-bashi, or tongs.

Japanese Inn

As well as private bathrooms, *ryokans* also have a large communal bath. People visit *ryokans* to enjoy the bath as much as to enjoy the food, and many *ryokans* boast luxurious bathhouses which attempt to create an atmosphere as close to nature as possible.

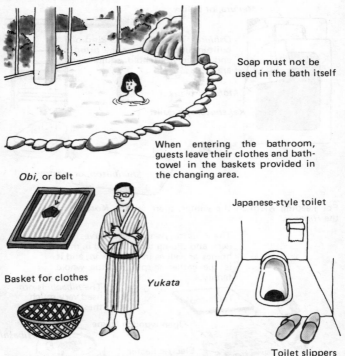

Soap must not be used in the bath itself

When entering the bathroom, guests leave their clothes and bathtowel in the baskets provided in the changing area.

Obi, or belt

Basket for clothes

Yukata

Japanese-style toilet

Toilet slippers

All the guest rooms in a *ryokan* are supplied with *yukata*, a kind of simple *kimono*, which can be worn around the *ryokan* for relaxing, or for going out for a walk, or for sleeping.

Breakfast and dinner are included in the price of a night's stay at a *ryokan,* and the maid brings both these meals to the guest rooms and serves them.

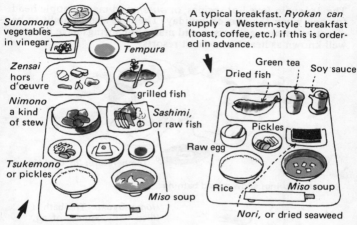

Sunomono vegetables in vinegar

Tempura

A typical breakfast. *Ryokan can* supply a Western-style breakfast (toast, coffee, etc.) if this is ordered in advance.

Zensai hors d'oeuvre

grilled fish

Nimono a kind of stew

Sashimi, or raw fish

Green tea

Dried fish

Soy sauce

Pickles

Raw egg

Tsukemono or pickles

Rice

Miso soup

Miso soup

Nori, or dried seaweed

Dinner in a *ryokan* may consist of *Kaiseki Ryōri,* *tempura,* or regional cooking. Beer, *sakē,* whisky and other drinks can be ordered separately.

The *Chōba* is the reception desk where the bill is paid. This is usually Western-style these days, and a traditional *chōba* is rarely seen.

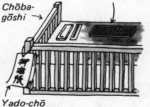

Abacus (*Soroban* in Japanese)

Chōba-gōshi →

Yado-chō

The bill is paid at the *Chōba* when leaving the *ryokan.* If a tip is given to the maid, this should be about five percent of the total.

温泉 Hot Spring

The Japanese love hot springs, or *onsen*, and many people head for one when they go on holiday. They are also thought to be effective in curing illnesses, and many hot springs have become well-known as health or tourist resorts.

Temperature: 25°C or above

Some hot springs allow mixed bathing

Types of hot spring treatment

Hōmatsuyoku. The bath is filled with bubbles of air, massaging the bather's whole body.

Utaseyu. The water from the hot spring is allowed to fall onto the bather's body from a height, massaging any painful or affected parts.

The *rotenburo*, or open-air bath, can be seen in various places around Japan. Its open, natural surroundings and calm, unhurried atmosphere are extremely relaxing.

Myōban Onsen (Ōita prefecture). This is famous for its *zabonburo*, where *zabon* (a type of orange) are put into the baths, increasing the latter's efficacy as a beauty treatment.

Mushiburo (Goshogake Onsen, Akita Prefecture) This is like a sauna, with steam entering through a pipe.

Sunamushiyu. (Ibusuki Onsen, Kagoshima pre-fecture). The bather steams his body by burying himself in hot sand.

167

駅弁 | Eki-ben

Ekiben are the box lunches sold in trains and stations all over Japan. They are cheap and convenient, and they usually contain some speciality of the area, making them very popular with travellers. They cost from five hundred to one thousand yen.

BENTO BENTŌ !

Eki-ben vendor

Green tea in a plastic container with cup. 60 yen.

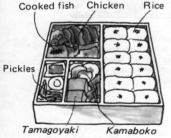

Cooked fish   Chicken   Rice

Pickles

Tamagoyaki   *Kamaboko*

Makunouchi-bentō

Makunouchi-bentō. This is the typical box lunch, originally sold in *Kabuki* theatres for the audience to eat during the intervals.

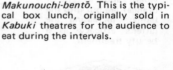

The three essential ingredients of a *makunouchi-bentō*:

- *Tamagoyaki*, a kind of sweet omelette
- *Kamaboko*, a cake made from steamed fish paste
- *Sakana*, raw or cooked fish

① *Ikameshi*, sold at *Mori* Station in *Hokkaidō*. This features squid, a speciality of Hokkaidō, stuffed with rice.

② *Kokeshi-bentō (Morioka* Station)

The container of this one is shaped like a * *kokeshi* doll.

Regional ekiben

④ *Kamameshi (Yokokawa* Station)

This is sold in a pottery *(Mashiko-yaki)* container.

③ *Imperial-bentō (Tōkyō* Station)

A box lunch containing both rice and bread.

⑥ *Fukumeshi (Shin-Shimonoseki* Station)

This contains *fugu*, or globefish, a speciality of *Shimonoseki*. The name *fukumeshi* is a play on words, since while *fugumeshi* might mean 'a meal of *fugu*', *fukumeshi* can be taken to mean 'a happy meal'.

⑤ *Hakkaku-bentō*(New *Ōsaka* Station)

This is a *makunouchi bentō* in an octagonal box, with the food cooked in the *Kansai* style.

* *Kokeshi* : See page 53.

新幹線　Shinkansen

The *Shinkansen*, Japan's famous 'bullet train', was inaugurated in October 1964 to coincide with the Tōkyō Olympics. The first line to be opened was the *Tōkaidō* Line.

Antenna for monitoring power-line voltage

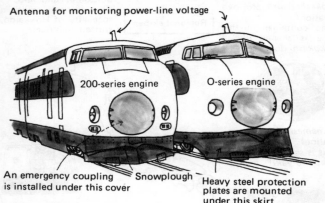

200-series engine

O-series engine

An emergency coupling is installed under this cover

Snowplough

Heavy steel protection plates are mounted under this skirt

The pantograph is pressed up against the overhead power lines by small springs. The part that contacts the wires must be replaced frequently.

The cyclone-type snow eliminators on the *Tōhoku Shinkansen*

There have been no passenger deaths on the *Shinkansen,* an exceptional safety record.

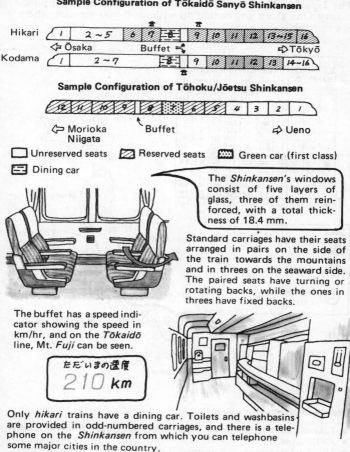

Sample Configuration of Tōkaidō Sanyō Shinkansen

Hikari | 1 | 2~5 | 6 | 7 | 8 | 9 | 10 | 11 | 12 | 13~15 | 16

⇦ Ōsaka   Buffet ⇄   ⇨ Tōkyō

Kodama | 1 | 2~7 | 8 | 9 | 10 | 11 | 12 | 13 | 14~16

Sample Configuration of Tōhoku/Jōetsu Shinkansen

12 | 11 | 10 | 9 | 8 | 7 | 6 | 5 | 4 | 3 | 2 | 1

⇦ Morioka   Buffet   ⇨ Ueno
Niigata

☐ Unreserved seats   ▨ Reserved seats   ▦ Green car (first class)
⊟ Dining car

> The *Shinkansen*'s windows consist of five layers of glass, three of them reinforced, with a total thickness of 18.4 mm.

Standard carriages have their seats arranged in pairs on the side of the train towards the mountains and in threes on the seaward side. The paired seats have turning or rotating backs, while the ones in threes have fixed backs.

The buffet has a speed indicator showing the speed in km/hr, and on the *Tōkaidō* line, Mt. *Fuji* can be seen.

ただいまの速度
210 km

Only *hikari* trains have a dining car. Toilets and washbasins are provided in odd-numbered carriages, and there is a telephone on the *Shinkansen* from which you can telephone some major cities in the country.

The Japanese National Railways are renowned for their punctuality. One thing you cannot do without if you are using them is a timetable.

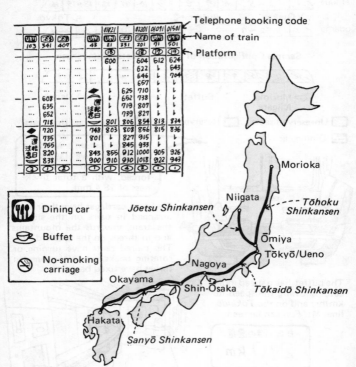

Telephone booking code
Name of train
Platform

Dining car

Buffet

No-smoking carriage

Morioka

Niigata

Jōetsu Shinkansen

Tōhoku Shinkansen

Ōmiya

Tōkyō/Ueno

Nagoya

Tōkaidō Shinkansen

Okayama

Shin-Ōsaka

Hakata

Sanyō Shinkansen

Names of Shinkansen trains

- *Tōkaido, Sanyō-Shinkansen Hikari* (Limited express) *Kodama* (Express)
- *Jōetsu-Shinkansen*   *Asahi* (Limited express)   *Toki* (Express)
- *Tōhoku-Shinkansen*   *Yamabiko* (Limited express)   *Aoba* (Express)

街の案内板 Signs & Signals

Most of the signs in Japan are naturally written in Japanese, but some are also in English or have some kind of illustration. Here are a few that will prove useful to know.

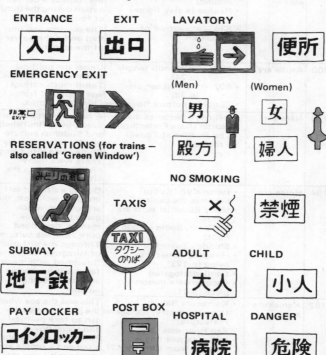

ENTRANCE
入口

EXIT
出口

LAVATORY

便所

EMERGENCY EXIT

非常口
EXIT

(Men)

男

殿方

(Women)

女

婦人

RESERVATIONS (for trains — also called 'Green Window')

みどりの窓口

NO SMOKING

禁煙

TAXIS

TAXI
タクシー
のりば

SUBWAY

地下鉄

ADULT

大人

CHILD

小人

PAY LOCKER

コインロッカー

POST BOX

〒

HOSPITAL

病院

DANGER

危険

173

付録　Supplement

CHRONOLOGICAL TABLE

Year AD	Era	Historical Event	Remarks
500	Yamato era	• Kofun (an ancient burial mound) • Haniwa (a clay figure) (p.52) • 538 — the arrival of Buddhism	Japan began to take the form of a unified nation during the third or fourth century. The country was unified under the power of the emperor.
600	Asuka era	• 593 — Shitennōji temple (p.24) • 607 — Hōryūji temple (p.24) • Buddhist culture flourishes	Under the political guidance of Shōtoku-Taishi much culture was imported from China and Korea.
710	Nara era	• Heijōkyō becomes the capital (Nara Prefecture) • The Buddha at Tōdaiji • Syōsōin	A nation with centralized power flourished and Buddhist culture heavily influenced by China came into being. There were many historic places in the city of Nara.
794	Heian era	• Heian-Kyō (Kyōto) becomes the capital • Many Buddhist sects are formed. • 1053 — Byōdōin Hōōdō is built. • Shinden Zukuri (p.9) • Hiragana comes into being (p.173) • Genji-monogatari • Lacquerware masterpiece (p.41)	During a state of self imposed seclusion, the aristocracy, which owned enormous manors, developed pure Japanese culture. Through the diffusion of Hiragana, literature flourished with many famous short poems and stories being written.
1192	Kamakura era	• Kamakura Bakufu (Kamakura city, Kanagawa Prefecture) • Zen flourishes (p.66) • India-ink painting is brought from China(p.42) • Many Bosatsu and Myō-ō idols are created (p.28) • Many Bonshō are made (p.29)	This was the age when the Samurai class began to take political and social power. Politeness was emphasized and a simple and sturdy spirit was respected.

Year AD	Era	Historical Event	Remarks
1336	Muromachi era	• Noh and Kyōgen are perfected (p.72) • Shoin-zukuri architecture (p.15, p.160) • Karesansui-style garden (p.15) • Ikebana (p.34), Cha-no-yu (p.30) • 1549 — arrival of Christianity	Kyōto, the capital, was burned down during fighting. Many aristocrats and samurai left for their home areas. Due to this fact, local culture thrived and the culture of the masses developed.
1573	Azuchi-momoyama era	• Many castles are built (p.17), Azuchi-jō castle, Ōsaka-jō castle • Thanks to Sen-No-Rikyū Cha-no-yu is perfected. (p.30)	This was the era in which Oda Nobunaga and Toyotomi Hideyoshi held political power and was also the age when grandiose, colorful culture developed.
1603	Edo era	• Christianity is banned. • Bunraku develops (p.75) • Himeji-Jō castle (p.18) • (1653 — 1724) Chikamatsu Monzaemon (p.70) • Katsura-Rikyū (p.14) • Nikkō Tōshōgū (p.20) • Kabuki and Ukiyoé are at their peak (p.48)	This was called the Tokugawa era. This era lasted for approximately 250 years from the time Tokugawa Ieyasu set up his government at Edo (Tōkyō).
1868	Meiji era	• Opening up of the country • Solar calendar • Railroad comes into use • Beginning of democracy • First use of electric transmission • The Tōkaidō Line is completed • Movies are imported	The country was opened up, capitalism was established and with the introduction of modern Western culture, the curtain was raised on a new era, one completely different from the previous Edo period.
1912	Taishō era	• 1914 — 1st World War • Political parties are at their peak • Literature for the masses • Women begin to enter society.	Capitalism reached maturity and the age of democracy became well established.
1926	Present era (Shōwa era)	• Shinkansen (p.168)	After the end of the second world war, rapid industrialization took place and Japan developed into one of the major economies of the world.

ADDITIONAL INFORMATION

1. Tradition And Culture

Buddhist temples and traditional architecture

Japan's traditional architecture centers around its Buddhist temples. Its structure, techniques and designs during the middle ages were all based on that of Buddhist temples. This was also present in the construction of shrines as well as private dwellings.

Periods during which the architecture of Buddhist temples in Japan was strongly influenced by Chinese architecture alternated with periods during which Japanization of that architecture took place. This pattern is found not only in architecture but in every aspect of Japan's traditional arts.

Via China and Korea, Buddhism first came to Japan in the middle of the sixth century. Starting with Prince *Shōtoku-taishi* (574 ∿ 622) successive rulers of Japan continued to import Buddhism. As a result, the *Shitennō-ji, Hōryū-ji* and many other Buddhist temples were built. Until the twelfth century, it was mainly only the ruling class that practiced Buddhism; however, Buddhism spread to the general populace in the 12th century. At the same time the practice of *Zen* Buddhism spread throughout Japan.

In the 12th and 13th centuries, *Zen* was brought to Japan by *Eisai* and *Dōgen*, Japanese priests who were studying in China. *Zen* was very well-suited to the Japanese spiritual and mental sensibilities and has become the backbone, as it were, of Japanese culture. In particular, it has had great influence on the arts which we have introduced in this book, such as *cha-no-yu, ikebana, budō* (martial arts), *noh, teien* (Japanese gardens) and Japanese pictures and writing in general.

Zen

Explained briefly, *Zen* involves using meditation to attain the ideal state of Buddhist salvation. Meditation is used to transcend all physical and emotional desires. One of the methods involved in this discipline is *Zazen*, which involves folding one's arms and legs and meditating with half an eye open. The doctrine of *Zen* Buddhism can best be described by the words of *Daruma,* the founder of *Zen* Buddhism. According to him, it is, "communication without words, expression without letters". In other words, truth is not expressed through words or knowledge, rather it is obtained and transmitted through direct experience. Therefore, those who practice *Zen* attempt to dissolve and transcend language and their own sense of values. Because of this, the communication between *Zen* priests is generally composed of "difficult to understand" catechetical questions and Buddhist catechisms.

Example of a Catechetical Question

"What is a path?"
"A path? A path would be that on the outside of the fence."
"I don't mean that sort of path. I'm talking about the spiritual main path."
"I see, the main path over there leading straight to the capital."

Shintō and shrines:

Although *Zen* is difficult for foreigners to understand, *Shintō*, the indigenous religion of Japan, is even more difficult. This is because *Shintō* has no founder and no bible. Rather than trying to logically understand and worship through *Shintō*, Japanese people, it seems, retain *Shintō* in the form of customs within their own psyches.

Shintō is a form of nature worship practiced by the Japanese people, who were originally an agriculturally oriented race. In *Shintō* there is an infinite number of gods. In 1870, the authorities made *Shintō* the national religion and at the same time bestowed godhood on the emperor. After the 2nd world war, ties between *Shintō* and the government were cut and each shrine became independent.

Many Japanese people visit shrines when their babies are born and are married with *Shintō* ceremonies. Also, those studying for entrance exams will pray or make their wish at *Shintō* Shrines. Visiting shrines at New Year is also an old tradition. The influence of *Shintō* can be seen in traditional festivals, major events throughout the year and in good luck charms. Today, however, rather than being a religious or intellectual entity, *Shintō* is no more than a convenient tradition in the daily lives of most Japanese people who have no one particular god.

Noh

Noh is the oldest form of Japanese formal theater. It is based on *Sarugaku* (lit. monkey plays), which are basically humorous impersonations. It was formed from *Kan-ami* and *Ze-ami* and was perfected in the 14th century. In contrast to *Kabuki* and *Bunraku*, which are theater for the masses, *Noh* was mainly for the warrior class (*samurai* class).

Dōjō-ji

A woman named *Kiyohimé* came to the temple looking for a travelling priest named *Anchin* who had promised to marry her but who had run away. The woman found *Anchin* hiding in the bell of the temple. Because of her intense devotion to her quest, the woman turned into a snake and just as she wrapped herself around the temple bell it melted and *Anchin* died as well.

Kabuki

Kabuki can be roughly divided into historical plays and genre plays concerning the life of common people during the *Edo* period.

There are eighteen types of especially popular plays, which are referred to as *Jūhachiban*. Here, we will introduce one of those eighteen, called *Shibaraku*. (Refer to the picture on page 70.)

— Shibaraku —

The setting is a shrine compound. Very bad men who had been terrorizing the neighborhood attacked a good young couple who had come to pay their respects to the shrine. They tried to kill the man and proceeded to do as they wished with the young wife. Just then a voice says the word *"shibaraku"* (just a moment), and the good hero makes his appearance. He then beats up the bad men where they stand.

Although the story is very simple, this is a work with many interesting highlights such as *Kumadori*, rich colourful costumes, animated movements, eloquent oratory and tricky acting.

Bunraku

Bunraku is a type of puppet theater that is sometimes referred to as *Ningyō-Jōruri*. The development of *Bunraku* parallels that of *Kabuki* and there are also some similar performances. The main feature is the elaborate dolls operated usually by three people, who wear black costumes and black hoods and are called *Kuroko*. *Kuroko* appear on stage but have no direct part in the story. The main acting is carried out by the dolls.

Kuroko

Although *Kuroko* appear in *Kabuki* and assist the actors, what is interesting is that the *Kuroko* are accepted to be invisible by the audience.

One of the best known of these plays is *Chikamatsu Monzaemon's* work, *Shinjū-Ten-No-Amijima*.

— Shinjū-Ten-No-Amijima —

A prostitute named *Koharu*, who lives in a place called Sonezaki, becomes very close to a regular customer by the name of *Jihei*. However, at the pleading of *Jihei's* wife *Osan*, the two are separated. In spite of her love for *Jihei*, *Koharu* agrees to be indentured to a rich man. As *Osan* knows that *Koharu* has decided to commit suicide, she collects money for *Jihei* himself to
---

> buy *Koharu's* indenture. Just then *Osan's* father comes to visit. He is disgusted at *Jihei's* behaviour and proceeds to take *Osan* back to his home. *Jihei* then takes *Koharu* to the temple at Amijima, where they pledge their love in the after life and commit suicide together.

This work is performed in both *Bunraku* and *Kabuki* and has even been made into a movie.

The background of this work is the *Yūkaku* (red light district) system which is difficult for foreigners to understand. *Yūkaku* often appears in Japan's plays and literature. We will explain this further here.

Yūkaku

The *Yūkaku* was a red light district in which prostitution was legal. (It was outlawed in 1958.) A unique society developed around the *Yūkaku* area and this has had a great influence on Japanese culture. Together with the theater, the *Yūkaku* district provided an important social pastime. Many of the women *(Yūjo)* who worked in the *Yūkaku* district, were very accomplished in the arts of *Bungei* (literary arts) and music. They were an integral feature of the art *(ukiyoé, kabuki, bunraku)* of the *Edo* Period.

The *Yūjo* were employed as indentured prostitutes until their emancipation (meaning ability to change professions) in 1872. They worked under the *Miuké* system. Under this system, unless they were able to pay a very high price they were not able to leave it. A lot of the *Shinjū-Mono* of *Bunraku* and *Kabuki*, derives from this type of background (tragedies in which a man and woman who are not allowed to consummate their love in this life will die together so that they can be united in the world after).

Art of the Masses

Devoted enthusiasts aside, all Japanese know at least a little about the various arts we have mentioned. In addition to those arts, there are others such as *Rakugo, Naniwabushi* and *Minyō*. These are the arts of the masses and were present in all parts of society.

Now we would like to briefly introduce a *Rakugo* work — *Toki-Soba*.

Toki-Soba

A man who has, while eating at the *soba* (noodle shop), been flattering the shop staff excessively asks for the bill. He says "All I have is very small coins". Then he proceeds to count 1, 2, 3 . . . . 7, 8 and asks "What time is it now?" The *Soba* man says "Nine" so he continues to count, 10, 11, 12 . . . In this way he deceives the *soba* shop owner.

Yotarō, watching this, tries to do the same thing the next day. He counts, "1, 2 . . 7, 8" then he asks, "What time is it now?" "Four", answers the shop owner. Then *Yotarō* continues to count 5, 6 . . . , and ends up paying more and losing out.

Tanka and Haiku

We have already introduced Japan's unique short poem forms, the *Tanka* and *Haiku* on page 65 of the text. Here, we would like to give a brief explanation of some basic concepts of Japanese literature. They are *"mono-no-awaré"*, *"wabi"* and *"sabi"*.

Mono-no-awaré

The *"Mono"* refers to nature, society, one's environment and destiny. *"Awaré"* indicates the heart which feels things very strongly. At the root of these concepts is the idea that nature and destiny are something that god has provided and cannot be changed or affected through human actions. This is based on a sense of nature which extends from a mythological age. In other words, before nature, the best that human beings could do was to enjoy and feel its beauty. It was believed that, for human beings to oppose nature or to try and change nature went against the will of god.

"Awaré" was considered to be the deepest and strongest emotion and was the basic human emotion. By understanding *"awaré"* it was believed that one would attain a closer harmony with nature, the eternal source of all things.

Wabi and Sabi

Japan's most representative poet is *Matsuo Bashō* who lived during the 17th century. According to him, *"Haiku is not something orthodox, rather it's something subtle and delicate."* Compared with the existing *Tanka* form, *Haiku* attempted to express human emotions in more detail. One of the fundamental concepts for expressing these emotions is the *Wabi* and *Sabi* concept. They are actually a taste for simplicity and tranquility refined into a pure art form. It is the idea that there is no such thing as waste. Something that is mentally beautiful exists within an old (nostalgic) and sad scene (feeling and emotion). This concept also exists in Japan's architecture and *cha-no-yu* traditions.

2. Japanese Life And Traditions

Dwellings

Modern Japanese dwellings are usually made of wood and are generally one or two stories high. In the major centers, many people live in reinforced concrete apartments, while many others live in narrow cramped rows of half Japanese, half western-style houses.

Today's average Japanese *"salaryman"* lives in a house with an area of 50 ~ 100 m². For people in western countries this may seem very small, but, because of the fact that the population of Japan is so concentrated in the cities, the land prices are too high to be able to afford better. A Japanese is very happy to simply attain his dream of owning his own home. The desire to possess one's own home is very strong and there is a growing number of people who will spend long hours commuting to work, just to own a home in the suburbs. The average price is 20 ~ 50 million yen (80 ~ 200 thousand dollars U.S.) for a 3 or 4 room apartment.

Tatami

Please refer to p. 8 ~ 13 of the text for the outward appearance of Japanese homes. Now we will explain *tatami* mats. Most characteristic of Japanese style rooms are the *tatami* mats on the floor. They are made of straw and rushes in measure approximately 180 x 90 cm. Japanese-style homes are made according to the number of mats being used per room (usually 4 and a half or 6).

Also please remember that in Japan one takes one's shoes off before entering the rooms of the house.

Jūnishi (The twelve horary signs)

Once upon a time, long ago, God in Heaven announced to all the animals that he would choose twelve from among them for a special task. That task would be for each animal, in turn, to protect human beings for one year. He told them that they should come to him on January 12 and that he would decide their order on a first come basis.

The animals waited eagerly for this day. However, it seems that the cat had for some time been very forgetful and did not remember the day himself. The cat ran into the rat along the way but the rat wanted to be first, so he told the cat that the day was the 13th.

When the rat returned home (his home was in the rafters of a barn) he saw the cow preparing to leave. "I'm so slow, I have to leave tonight or I'll never get there on time," he said.

Then, the rat who was very cunning had a clever idea. He concealed himself on the cow's back among her things. They travelled all night until they reached God's palace. The cow was very happy thinking that she would be the first but, just then the rat jumped in front of her, and the cow ended up second.

The next day the cat came hurrying to the palace but alas, even though the cat knew he had been deceived by the rat, he was left out of the group of twelve animals.

It is because of this that cats and rats, to this day, do not get along.

INDEX

Both English and Japanese terms, with the Japanese characters for the latter, are listed in the index below.

191

ILLUSTRATED
A LOOK INTO JAPAN

英文　日本絵とき事典 1

初 版 発 行　　1984年3月20日
改訂13版　　　1988年3月20日
　　　　　　　（Mar. 20, 1988 13th edition）

編　集　人　　斉藤晃雄
発　行　人　　木下幸雄
発　行　所　　日本交通公社出版事業局
　　　　　　　〒101 東京都千代田区神田鍛冶町3-3
　　　　　　　大木ビル8階(Tel. 03-257-8391)
　　　　　　　海外ガイドブック編集部
印　刷　所　　交通印刷株式会社

編集制作　　株式会社アーバン・トランスレーション
イラスト　　松下正己
表紙デザイン　東芳純
翻　　訳　　John Howard Loftus
　　　　　　William Harland

交通公社発行図書のご注文は
日本交通公社出版販売センター
〒101 東京都千代田区神田須田町1-12
　山萬ビル 8 階(Tel.03-257-8337)
　振替　東京7-99201　送料(実費共)225円

定価 880円

873424　　712020
ISBN4-533-00307-9 C2026 ¥880E